Holding Pattern

Airport
Waiting
Made
Easy

HARRY KNITTER

Kordene Publications, Ltd.
Okemos, Michigan

Published by Kordene Publications, Ltd.
4463 Copperhill, Okemos, Michigan 48864.

Publisher's Cataloging-in-Publication Data
Knitter, Harry W.
  Holding pattern: airport waiting made easy / Harry Knitter — Okemos, Michigan. : Kordene Publications, Ltd., c1996.
    p.   ill.   cm.
  Includes index.
  ISBN 0-9652333-0-8
  1. Air travel. 2. Travelers—Recreation. 3. Games for travelers. I. Title.
G151.K57   1996
910.2—dc20   96-76138

PROJECT COORDINATION BY JENKINS GROUP, INC.

99 98 97 ❖ 5 4 3 2 1

Printed in the United States of America

To Kayla and Nicholas

CONTENTS

PREFACE

When I was an impressionable boy of 7 or 8, my dad often occupied our Sunday afternoons by driving my brother Jim and me over to the perimeter road encircling Billy Mitchell Field in Milwaukee. He'd park our old '39 Lincoln Zephyr near the airport fence, facing it perpendicular to the runway, so we could sit on the running board and watch the planes of the '40's take off. Each time we looked down the length of the narrow runway and listened to the vibrating roar of the old propeller-driven engines as they struggled to lift the aircraft up and over our heads, I thought about being on board someday, flying off to distant destinations and meeting people from far-off lands. Like many young people from non-traveling families of modest means, I never dreamed that I'd ever actually realize my fantasies.

Since my dad left this earth over 35 years ago, I never got to tell him about my many air travel experiences. In my business career, I've logged over a million miles in the air on trips to

Europe, South America, Bermuda, Puerto Rico, South Africa, Hawaii, Mexico, and Canada—and to most of the 50 United States. And as you might imagine, I've spent hundreds of hours in airports—in a holding pattern.

This book is my way of sharing the experiences of almost 40 years of travel. It's designed to help you take airport delays in stride, to use the time in an entertaining and intelligent way, and to exercise and stretch the mind. In some of the chapters, we'll also exercise the body, as well as your purse or billfold. And, in the final chapters, you'll learn techniques to help you prepare for future travel.

If you come away from this experience feeling better and finding yourself mentally and physically refreshed—eagerly looking forward to your next flight—then I've accomplished my goal.

If you don't, I'll be the first to tell you to stay away from sleeping pills and silverware. You may be a hopelessly depressed basket case who's better off staying home, where you won't infect more than your immediate family.

ACKNOWLEDGMENTS

A book of any kind is an awesome undertaking for a first-time author.

One of the major challenges is resisting the temptation to start out with a boring set of acknowledgments, and—to be candid—that opening sentence above gets this one off to an extraordinarily dull, snoozy start.

Let me begin again, so I can tell you how I truly feel:

I need to be discreet in acknowledging anyone in this book, because most people who became aware of my intent to write it tried desperately to talk me out of it. As you can tell, I ignored their advice and plunged recklessly ahead despite their repeated attempts to hide my computer mouse. My wife Nancy deserves to be thanked for her enthusiastic support; on the other hand, this project got me out of her hair for four hours a night, week after grueling week, and for some reason she's smiling a lot more these days.

I appreciate the support my boys—Scott, Dave, and Andy—gave me, but if they thought they'd get away without being pressured to hawk a few hundred books among their friends and co-workers, Fat Chance. And, dear daughter-in-law Leslie: Don't forget to hit up those frequent-flying clients for a dozen or two orders!

As for Mike and Jan Hogan and Doug and Lu Hagemann, close friends, not a single one of them thought I could pull this off—and still won't believe it until I'm interviewed on *Oprah.* Jerry Jenkins and Mark Dressler of The Jenkins Group promised they'd get me on, but both of them have recently stopped answering my phone calls, so I may have to settle for *Tool Time* instead.

The coolest heads on this prolonged project belonged to Alex Moore, production editor, and Andrew Toos, cartoonist. I'd say you're the greatest, guys, but I've only produced this one book, so maybe we should settle for "great."

I'd like to send my thanks and condolences to my friends and associates at The John Henry Co.—especially Brenda Copley, Jim Doll, and Marina Hawkins, who served as sounding boards and test cases. They have to put up with my wierd sense of cornball humor every working day. You can extinguish it by finishing this book. . . or by escaping onto your next flight.

Finally, I'm indebted to Professor Linda Peckham of Lansing Community College, whose classes have been a source of inspiration to hundreds of aspiring writers for over 20 years. Linda provided the encouragement to launch this project and her tactful guidance kept it from falling off the shelf time and again.

Thanks to all of the above for helping me do this gig.

And, thanks to you for making it all worth doing.

After all, it's the last time in my life I'll be a first-time author.

PART I
Food For Thought

There's no need to be rattled over your sudden predicament. You'll be better off if you pause and think about the positive things you could accomplish during the next minutes or hours.

1.

Just A Temporary Setback

Thou art indeed just, Lord, if I contend
With thee; but, sir, so what I plead is just
Why do sinners' ways prosper? and why must
Disappointment all I endeavour end?

— Horace

It's a sudden, depressing let-down experienced sooner or later by every air traveler. One minute you're expecting to jet away into the clouds, and the next minute you're stuck on the ground for an indefinite period of time. No matter how frequently you travel, one day the cacophony of gibberish spewing from the flight terminal loud speaker system contains the one announcement you're least prepared to deal with at that moment:

> *Attention, passengers on flight 241 to Des Moines. That flight has been cancelled due to mechanical difficulties. Passengers are requested to report to the agents at Gate 23 for rebooking on an alternative flight.*

15

It's 7:30 on a Friday evening, and you know there isn't another aircraft leaving for Des Moines (or wherever you're heading) until 10:50 p.m. You go through the motions of rebooking the last available seat with a minimum of enthusiasm, knowing you're going to be left with three hours to "kill" at a time when the airport is loaded with travelers. What do you do now?

Like many typical travelers caught in the "hold" mode, you

could head for the nearest doughnut shop or cinnamon bun coffee bar and gorge yourself on calories that'll feel like a stomach full of lead sinkers the rest of the evening. Or you could enjoy hours of stimulating, entertaining activities that will exercise your mind and/or your body, leaving you refreshed and ready to finish your day on a positive note.

This book is written for the growing masses of air travelers, like you and me, who find themselves waiting in the world's bustling airline terminals without an organized plan to use the unanticipated luxury of loose time.

It's estimated that congestion lengthened "dwell time" in airports by about 5% per year in the 1990's, according to *The Wall Street Journal*.   That leaves the typical domestic air traveler with an *average* of 59 minutes in the delay mode, per airport visit, because of late or cancelled flights, connection problems, and normal layover time, reports Air Marketing Services, a consulting firm in White Plains, N.Y.

As a marketing executive with Chrysler, FTD, and The John Henry Co., I've been a frequent flyer for most of my adult life. Whether on business or pleasure trips, I've spent what, in retrospect, seems to be years of waking hours ruminating in airport terminals, waiting impatiently for flights that were delayed or cancelled and rebooked with substitute aircraft.   Some of my experiences bordered on the bizarre.

One morning in Kansas City, I boarded a flight to Chicago and settled comfortably into my seat with a couple of morning papers, anticipating a pleasant one-hour trip to O'Hare, where I was scheduled to connect with a commuter flight taking me home to Lansing, Michigan.   All preparatory activity on the plane seemed to be in routine order until the captain's voice announced the following:

> *Ladies and gentlemen, we're privileged to have a special guest in our cockpit for this morning's flight: a smiling fellow who identified himself as an FAA inspector. We're*

happy to have him on board to check us out and make sure we're complying with all of the regulations as we prepare to get you safely to Chicago. That's the good news.

*As he performed his prescribed checks, however, the inspector discovered that our young copilot has somehow neglected to have his license accompany him on board this morning. Since he can't legally fly without it, he's now on his way by taxicab to downtown Kansas City, where he lives, to pick up the missing license and return immediately to the cockpit so we can get on our way. When he arrives back on board, I'll let **him** explain why he caused all of us to change our schedules on this otherwise bright and cheerful morning.*

True to his word, upon the copilot's return, the pilot put him on the intercom and sat back while the embarrassed sidekick sheepishly apologized, in the unsteadiest of voices, for his gaffe. We went on our way shortly after everyone in the cabin joined in a chorus of boos. . . following a round of free booze in the form of Bloody Marys and mimosas, served to soothe our impatient nerves.

If you've flown for any length of time, you've probably encountered more unexpected delays than you'd like to remember.

At Washington's Dulles Airport a couple of years ago, my wife and I were waiting to board a jumbo jet destined for Madrid,

Spain, where we were scheduled to connect with a flight to Valencia for a business conference. As departure time neared, the boarding area became a sea of confusion, with waves of Hispanics crowding around the service counter. Their harried, English-speaking travel agent was trying her best to distribute tickets and seat assignments to members of the group, but the mob of chattering, well-wishing relatives and other bystanders in the gate area made order and organization totally impossible. Finally, she managed to distribute the last of the tickets and the gate agents initiated the boarding process.

Now running at least an hour late, we thought we had seen the worst. Uh, uh.

The worst was witnessing an outbreak of general chaos in the economy cabins as members of the Spanish-speaking group decided unilaterally that they wanted to sit with their friends. . . ignoring the seat assignments on their boarding passes. Then the plot became even thicker when the flight crew realized they didn't have an accurate passenger count, and several people were still unaccounted for.

Out of total confusion came this announcement, at long last:

*This is the captain speaking. We cannot and **will not** leave this airport tonight until everyone is in their assigned seat and we have completed an accurate count of passengers. We **will not** depart until this is accomplished.*

Finally, the wayward fliers and social gadabouts heeded the somber message and a semblance of order was restored so that we could take off—now almost two hours late. Order was maintained through the night as we crossed the Atlantic, only to erupt into massive confusion once again in the baggage claim area following our arrival on Spanish soil. But you get the picture.

On most air trips, planes leave and arrive on time. But when delays occur, they're almost always longer than the gate agents project them to be. That's one reason some airlines communicate the anticipated new departure time reluctantly. They don't want to be committed to a time estimate they know will likely be inaccurate.

Delayed and cancelled flights cause greater anxiety at night than earlier in the day because there's a shorter time window in which to facilitate alternative remedies.

And people are more tired and cranky as the day winds down—including gate agents.

Moreover, passengers become increasingly concerned, at that point, with the possibilities of an unplanned stayover, requiring a change of clothes, a toiletry kit, and arrangements for nearby hotel accommodations. Unexpected overnighters are especially awkward to handle when the luggage has already been checked and may not be available. That's why it's a good idea to keep a travel kit and change of clothes in a carry-on bag, just in case (no pun intended).

Whatever you do, think about alerting your family and/or company that your itinerary has changed, and let them know where you are in case of emergency. If you're going to miss a meeting with a customer, contact them immediately to make them aware that your travel plans are on hold. Besides being a good idea, a phone conversation with someone familiar will provide comfort when you find yourself in a far-off airport.

You might also think about calling your travel agent to check out alternative flight availabilities. Their computer link with all the airlines that fly out of the city in which you're stranded will probably turn up more options than you'll get from the harried gate agent, whose attention is split dozens of different ways at this moment.

If, after a while, you suspect something extraordinary is going on and that you're not getting the straight story from the gate agent, ask him or her to "240" you. That means you're requesting that they invoke Rule 240 of their contract of carriage; in essence, it requires them to cover any additional expense incurred in having another carrier get you to your planned destination. Have them indicate the code on your ticket, and present the ticket to the alternate carrier (having checked in advance that they fly to that city and have room for you).

After completing that process, return to these pages and enjoy a full cabin of tips designed to help you spend your uncommitted time doing interesting things. Not the least of them, hopefully, will be reliving some of my travel and business experiences with me.

2.

Lighten Up
Keeping Cool is Cool

If you can keep your head when all about you
Are losing theirs and blaming it on you.
If you can trust yourself when all men Doubt you,
But make allowances for their doubting too;
If you can wait and not be tired by waiting.
                                    —Rudyard Kipling

Unexpected delays in airports call for a positive attitude rather than a needless state of depression while you wait, immersed in a vacuum of information. It's one of those times when you must convince yourself to view the situation as the proverbial "glass half full" rather than "half empty." While it may seem that you have lost control of the present situation (and you have), there are many ways in which you can regain your equilibrium and manage to make lemonade out of the lemon flight schedule that has just fallen off the tree into your lap.

Stranded by a so-called cancelled flight at the Ft. Lauderdale airport one early Sunday morning in February, I received a club room pass, a fast and comfortable limousine ride to the Miami airport, a premium seat assignment on a later flight, and free drink tickets to make the alternative flight home easier to swallow.

I've always found that a constructive, low-key negotiating approach works best with harried counter and gate agents at a time when you need their empathy and support. Blustering and counter-pounding are out.   Calm, common sense logic are in. Your best leverage is an admission by the airline that *they* messed up your trip plans.

As you deal with your moment of frustration, be sure to recognize that the airline company and its flight crew want you to be on your way safely and on schedule as much as you do. Their reputation and on-time record are at stake. But they can't get you on your way for one of these reasons: 1) mechanical problems need to be solved; 2) they're awaiting a member of the flight crew; 3) Air Traffic Control is holding up the departure because of heavy traffic; or 4) someone just made an honest mistake.

In the Ft. Lauderdale scenario I started to describe above, I had arrived with bloodshot eyes, before sunrise, at the airport, turned in my rental car, and stepped off the shuttle van at about 6:05 for a 6:45 a.m. flight. The baggage claim curb agent took my ticket, frowned, and promptly informed me that the flight on which I was booked had been cancelled due to a storm in Charlotte, North Carolina, the first scheduled stop on my journey back to Michigan. I retrieved my bags quickly, hustled into the terminal, and began a search of alternative flights. Finding another airline's flight about to leave for Chicago, I went on standby —but the flight was oversold and there were no seats available.

So, out of breath, I trudged back to the original airline's ticket counter to rebook for a later flight. The counter agent looked at my ticket, glanced at the clock, and said, "Why didn't you get on your ticketed flight?"

When I recounted my earlier conversation with the curb agent, the counter person checked the schedule sheet that had been furnished to the baggage-handler and concluded that the curb agent had mistakenly referred to the previous day's listing. *Today's* conditions were actually much improved and the flight I had been booked on left on schedule from Ft. Lauderdale. Their blunder had caused the predicament in which I found myself at that moment. **Gotcha!**

After expressing her airline's sincere apologies, the agent began the task of searching for another seat for me on a later flight. Because of storms through the northeast that weekend, however, there were none available from Ft. Lauderdale. Working aggressively on her computer to resolve my dilemma, she found an open seat on a flight leaving the Miami airport in about three hours—**First Class** accommodations, no less. She asked if I would mind taking a prepaid limo ride to Miami, a trip of about 45 minutes.

"But that still leaves me with two hours to kill in Miami, and I'll be arriving in Detroit almost six hours later than with my original connections," I responded. She nodded, shrugged her shoulders and apologized once again.

Then, reaching into a drawer, she located a day pass for the VIP lounge at the Miami airport and calmed my anxiety further by producing a handful of free drink coupons good on future flights.

Ah, the value of leverage. It works almost every time.

When I've had the misfortune to experience a cancellation late at night, causing an unplanned overnight stay, I've always found the airlines do their best to maintain goodwill. They usually provide vouchers for rooms and meals at the nearest hotels, free limo or cab service, and a confirmed flight the next morning. Of course, if the airline is at fault for your predicament, you should be able to get basic supplies like a razor and toothbrush from them at no charge, or at least arrange for reimbursement of any expenses you incur if an overnight stay is needed. The operative word to be uttered frequently in this situation is "voucher."

Keep your cool when everyone else is ranting and raving, and strategically push for every possible concession the airline agent is authorized to grant to relieve your frustration. In most circumstances, they'll come through handsomely if you approach the problem with tact and respect for their position. If they don't, ask to speak with their supervisor. He or she will have broader authority to compromise on your requests.

One type of experience you will want to especially avoid happened recently to a friend of mine. He was on a flight that stopped in Pittsburgh and was scheduled to continue on to Toronto. During the Pittsburgh stop, the crew announced that mechanical problems were being worked on and that the anticipated layover time of 30 minutes could stretch out to an *hour* and 30 minutes or so. Most of the passengers going on to Toronto, including my friend, deplaned to get some exercise and stop for a sandwich and beer.

While he was in the coffee shop, my friend Mike became engrossed in a basketball game on the tube and inadvertently missed the announcement that his flight was departing just a few minutes behind schedule—not an hour late, as originally indicated by the on board crew. The repairs had been completed earlier than anticipated and, in their zeal to stay close to their schedule, the airline released the flight without Mike—whose $4,000 laptop computer and business papers were in his carry-on bag in the overhead compartment.

There's a two-part moral to this story:

1. **Never leave valuables aboard a flight when you deplane during a stopover.**

2. **Never put much stock into the airline's first announcements of anticipated departure time. Their projected departure times are almost always hedged "guesstimates" that don't hold up when the actual departure decisions are made and carried out.**

When you first learn your flight has been delayed or cancelled, follow these steps, in this order of priority:

1. **Get all the information you can collect from the airline's counter person;**

2. **Call your travel agent and ask him or her to find alternative flight arrangements for you (most agencies have a toll-free hot line number you'll find on your trip itinerary in the ticket jacket).**

3. **If you can't reach your agent, call the airline directly (major airline numbers are listed in Appendix I) and check out alternative flight availabilities. Don't waste your time in line at**

the counter when you could be talking directly to the airline and be plugged into the best available information bank.

4. If you're within reasonable driving distance of your ultimate destination, consider booking a rental car as soon as you find out your next flight has been delayed or cancelled. With a reservation in hand, you'll have alternative transportation to fall back on if your airline arrangements fall apart.

Do it by phone; if you try to make reservations at the rental desk, they'll probably want you to fill in the paperwork and pick up the car.

By making car reservations early on, you won't have to race the crowd to the rental counters, leaping wildly over rows of waiting area seats, when the "cancelled" message finally turns up on the TV monitors. Of course, if your flight does materialize eventually, don't forget to cancel your car reservation—by Airphone, if you forgot to handle that chore while in the terminal. Toll-free phone numbers of major rental car agencies are listed in Appendix III.

By using your IQ rather than your uncontrolled emotions to make decisions during these anxious moments, you'll make a lot more progress and, at the same time, constrain your stress level under the overload stage while you're trying to get back on track after your flight arrangements fall apart.

Lighten up and try to maintain your poise and composure. There's something pathetic about a normally rational human being going berserk at a check-in counter and verbally abusing a petite 5-foot, 1-inch 26-year-old agent who's trying her best to be helpful. Use logic and reason to identify those things you can control—don't sweat about the things you *can't* control—and soon you'll be back on your journey, smiling about the experience you survived without a foolish, emotional burnout.

Most people, including me, feel their stress level rise in noisy, crowded, uncomfortable conditions—so look for a quiet, uncrowded gate area where you can relax and cool off. (Don't forget to stay within earshot of the public address announcements, however, so you can hear updates on your flight status).

Every day, the world will provide you with plenty of reasons for stress and anxiety; therefore, it just makes sense to avoid creating additional nerve-stretchers on your own. Be cool. Two weeks from now your frustrating experience will seem like a trivial episode from the past.

3.

There's No
Time To Waste

O let not Time deceive you,
You cannot conquer Time.

— W.H. Auden

If there's no practical alternative to simply waiting out the situation, face the challenge of "killing" a few hours with a realistic view: You might as well make the most of the extra time you've just been handed rather than sitting in the gate area, transfixed as if in a comatose condition. Assess your options, and then invest the first few minutes in the formulation of a creative strategy to use your free time productively and enjoyably.

If you're an avid reader, here's your opportunity to catch up on that book you've been carrying around for the past six months. Or how about hunting down the interesting novel you heard about on that talk show earlier in the week? Air terminal bookstores are loaded with the latest bestsellers.

Some airport book outlets carry the works of local authors, providing you with the opportunity to discover fine writers who

31

might otherwise remain unknown. At the Minneapolis-St. Paul terminal, for example, you'll find an exceptionally good used bookstore, stocked with a wide variety of titles at heavily-discounted prices.

But the best choice in terminals for avid readers is the Book Cellar at the Raleigh-Durham (North Carolina) airport, where you'll have more than 16,000 used books to choose from. The selection ranges from the classics, collections on military history, and volumes by Southern writers, to sections featuring mysteries and children's books.

And, if you're stuck in Raleigh-Durham after the bookstore closes, never mind.

The Book Cellar policy is to display several racks of books outside the store and people pay on the honor system. (Believe it or not, customers actually *pay* for the books they take, which must say something for the moral standards of travelers in need of reading material).

According to a recent survey published in *U.S.A. Today*, 80% of the 1,100 frequent flyers responding said they read while waiting for their flights. Another 73% said they "watch people"; 52% eat and/or drink; 48% shop; and 29% watch planes take off and land (respondents were able to check more than one activity). What do *you* like to do while you're waiting between flights?

Got a pad of paper and pen or pencil? Maybe this is a good time to write a letter to those close friends who moved out-of-state a year ago—you know, the ones you promised to keep in touch with, but just haven't had the time to call or write? Wouldn't it be fun to bring them up-to-date on what you've been doing during the past year—the places you've been to, the things you've done since you last saw them? Who knows, your letter might actually motivate them to give you a call and set a date to get together!

My wife's friend Janet, stranded in the Cincinnati airport (which isn't located in Cincinnati, but in Covington, Kentucky), decided on a lark to phone an old high school boyfriend she knew had relocated to the Queen City some years back. Although they hadn't seen each other in a long time, the two old friends struck up a lively phone conversation that revealed, among other juicy tidbits, that he had been recently divorced and was now dating once again. Taking the cue, Janet arranged to meet him for breakfast the next morning and, after a few more chummy rendezvous over the next few months, they wound up committing to a breakfast with each other every morning for the rest of their lives.

You may not discover the love of your life during a flight delay, but you could find it an opportunity to renew a friendship or initiate a chat with a family member you haven't talked with in years. It's worth the investment of a couple of dollars in phone charges.

The secret is to find something productive and mentally stimulating to do. In my experience, most terminals have been designed to provide you with lots of entertaining and educational things you can explore during your waiting time. Why not take advantage of their available facilities by getting out and about while you've got the minutes or hours to "kill" before your next takeoff?

If you're so inclined, you might consider visiting one of the many chapels that exist in airports. They either offer a variety of multi-denominational services or are available for a few minutes of contemplative reflection on life and its challenges.

At Kennedy Airport in New York, for example, you'll find special icons of a domed building, representing a house of worship, on signs throughout the international terminal. Chicago O'Hare has a chapel on the mezzanine level of Terminal 2 , while Seattle offers a meditation room in the main terminal. Miami provides a lounge for meditation between concourses C and D.

There are more than 70 chapels in airports worldwide. The latest to be opened is at Denver International, where both a non-denominational chapel and adjacent Islamic prayer room are available to visitors. The Islamic facility, a prayer hall facing toward Mecca, is thought to be the first in an airport outside of the Islamic world.

4.

The Flight That Never Was

All the world's a stage,
And all the men and women merely players
— William Shakespeare

$\longmapsto$ $\mathbf{I}$f you've ever waited impatiently on board an airliner, while it was being held on the ground until a gate became available or while it was in line behind 20 other jets preparing to take off, you know when it happens that it seems you're on an interminable flight to nowhere. The minutes drag on, and you begin to feel that the whole trip is turning into a bad dream.

I spent most of a day on a plane that actually *was* going nowhere, but it was *planned* that way and everyone on board got paid for enduring the experience. Back in January of 1982, my boss at FTD and I spent a full day aboard a 747 parked at a gate at the Newark airport—and we weren't even upset. In fact, we were grateful.

The advertising agency for the airline had selected Bill, the executive vice-president of FTD, to appear in a TV commercial

35

for the airline company. The spot was one of a series of commercials being targeted toward their business customers, with contrived parallels drawn between the businesses being represented and the point the airline attempted to drive home in each spot.

In our case, for example, the commercial was designed to convey the message that FTD was in the business of delivering flowers on time anywhere in the world, drawing a parallel with the sponsoring airline as the carrier known for delivering passengers on-time anywhere the airline flew. Thus, FTD's respected worldwide flower delivery service was used as a means of dramatizing the airline's reliability and on-time record.

The spot opened on a scene in the first class cabin of the jumbo jet. The camera traveled down the aisle, panning over the faces of the nameless actors who were dressed like typical business people on a typical business trip. Finally, it zoomed in for a tight shot of Bill, who then spoke the critical opening line about FTD's on-time floral delivery service.

The scene occupied all of 15 seconds of air time on the final commercial, but it required almost a full day of setup, rehearsals, dry run-throughs, and about 35 "takes" before the director was happy with what he saw on his video playback machine.

Throughout all of this show-biz activity, the meter was running on the use of the 747, and the cost of keeping it out of service for that length of time must have been astronomical. But hey, this is the ad biz, and costs aren't much of a concern when a creative concept is being executed.

Another demonstration of the client's deep pockets took place in filming the second scene of the commercial. The sequence was shot on location in a New York floral shop, and it showed Bill standing in front of a cooler full of flowers. As the scene opened, the camera scanned the foreground displays and quickly moved in on Bill so he could deliver a brief line about the airline's on-time performance.

In order to create the setting, the agency had laid out big money to rent the 2nd Avenue Manhattan shop for five days. On Sunday and Monday, their crews completely gutted the shop, moving merchandise and fixtures out onto moving vans, while trucks carrying new shelving, counters, and coolers were being unloaded. Once the new fixtures were in place, they filled the setting with flowers and live plants, plus the normal accoutrements of a floral shop, like baskets, brass containers, and the like. Then they installed lighting, camera tripods, and other necessary equipment for the shoot, which occupied much of Tuesday. On Wednesday and Thursday, they moved the replacement fixtures and props back out of the shop and restored its original look with the old "stuff" and some fresh flowers. All of this action took place for a scene that occupied less than 10 seconds on the commercial when it aired.

The final scene showed Bill back on the plane handing his rose boutonniere to a smiling stewardess. The shooting of that episode consumed the time remaining on Monday afternoon, while the paid actors were still perched in the seats behind him.

Naturally, we were pleased to be featured in the commercial. It gave our association brand valuable national exposure during the important spring flower-buying period without costing us a single dollar. Our expenses for the trip were covered by the airline. And Bill even got paid for his part in the commercial with airline credits worth first-class upgrades on his future flights. As you might imagine, we weren't the least bit upset with the fact that our Newark 747 never even got its engine started. It was one time when we wished that we could have been "grounded" again and again.

PART II
Action And Interaction

You get to take part in stories and quizzes, or get on your feet for a little shopping, as well as other interesting exploits. Are you up to some exercise?

5.

Let's Make A Deal

Two voices are there: one is of the deep;
And one is of an old half-witted sheep
Which bleats articulate monotony.

— J. K. Stephen

In case you may not have no-
ticed, the robot-like voices that drone on, spewing out mundane
information on the airport terminal public address systems, lack
even the slightest evidence of human warmth and personality.
Agree?

Then perhaps you'll support my contention that, for the
sake of variety, the public address duties should occasionally
be turned over to someone with experience in another announc-
ing field. Say, for example, disk jockeys, sports announcers . . .
or car dealers. That's it—wheeling and dealing "automotive
purchase consultants."

Here's what the announcements might sound like, under
new ownership:

> *"Hi folks, this is Wally Wondersales—your*
> *close-to-home public address announcer*
> *bringing the best gosh darn information your*

hard-earned money can buy. And you get it today only at O'Hare International airport, conveniently located on the corner of Illinois Route 72 and the Tri-State 294.

"If you're in the market for excitement, just look out the terminal window, where your uncle Adam's shiny new Buick is being towed away by Sheriff Cook, while the good uncle is there at the terminal entrance, waving you good-bye. Well, be sure to tell him we've got plenty of low-mileage used cars just right for him and his lovely lady friend.

"Looking for special attention? Just leave your luggage bag unattended and our anti-terrorist training squad will slip a one-of-a-kind live grenade in the bag faster than you can say, 'What was that announcement? Did he say we shouldn't leave our gag *unattended?'*

"You want action? Then you and the missus will love this special, good today only: For only one day of the entire year, that's today folks, all flights scheduled at gate 1A1 have been moved to gate 79, just an easy walk of a mile or two down this corridor.

"But don't be discouraged, 'cause Wally's out to get you the right deal. Come and see

me personally, folks, and I'll do whatever it takes to put you into a genuine, one-owner golf cart, with good rubber, rich vinyl upholstery, a sturdy luggage rack, and a stereo beeping system that scares the daylights out of pedestrians in the concourses when we come rollin' in.

"It also comes with its own professional hot-rod porter who wouldn't mind scooping up a few aisle walkers with his specially-designed front end stainless steel plow blade.

"And don't forget the extra value feature we're offering on our mobile carts at no

extra charge this week only: Dual computer-activated "O'Hare bags" in the front dash panel that'll inflate to keep the missus from landing face first on the shiny terrazzo floors in the concourse should we encounter another cart or maybe one o' dem mobile newsstands.

"When it's time for your tip, don't worry if you're a little short of cash. We offer easy payments with nothing down and $3.00 a month for seven years. And you're automatically approved if you can walk through our doorway, are breathin', and can sign your name.

"That's it for now, folks. See us too-day! Bon voy-age."

Somehow, life in the terminal may never again seem the same.

*   *   *

If you had a choice, who would you like to see selected as a spokesman on the airport intercom system? _____

_____

What would he or she sound like? _____

_____
_____
_____
_____
_____
_____
_____
_____
_____
_____
_____

(My own preference would be the venerable Harry Caray, baseball announcer extraordinaire. Can you imagine his commentary on the comings and goings of travelers through an airport terminal? Or how about Dick Vitale, Baby? Then again, I think I'm at the point where a good 60-second T.O. would settle me back on track.)

6.

A Three-Letter Lingo

*We should constantly use the most
common, little, easy words (so they are pure
and proper) which our language affords.*

— John Wesley

While you wait for your flight to be called, have you noticed that baggage tags have a language all their own? Like the computer world, where terms like RAM and bytes confuse the neophytes, airline folks have created a destination lingo that may seem like gibberish to everyone in the airport—except baggage-handlers and check-in gate agents.

If your tag carries the symbol <u>ALO</u>, for example, it isn't meant to be a subtle greeting to the shapely blonde checking in just ahead of you in line. It means that bag (and, hopefully, its owner) is headed for Waterloo, Iowa. <u>ATH</u> doesn't tell the world you're an accomplished athlete, but that you're destined for Athens, Greece. And if you're wondering why everyone is putting plenty of distance between themselves and that innocent-looking fellow across the concourse, his bag tag may very well be the reason.

47

In case you haven't noticed, the abbreviation <u>BOM</u> is not an appropriate label to be displayed in an airport; it's simply an indication that the poor man is traveling to Bombay, India. He'd probably also prefer not to be labeled with the tag from Fresno, California, which proclaims that he'd be destined to land in <u>FAT</u>. (A suburb of Cholesterol, no doubt).

Celebrity-watchers might want to be on the lookout for <u>ITO</u> (Hilo, Hawaii) in hopes of catching a glimpse of the judge himself. Could that be Jay Leno with the bag labeled <u>LAF</u>? No, it's a friendly Hoosier heading for Lafayette, Indiana.

How many destination cities can you identify from this list of major airport codes in the U.S.?

1. ORD: _____

2. ATL: _____

3. DTW: _____

4. LGA: _____

5. LAX: _____

6. SLC: _____

7. WAS: _____

8. EWR: _____

9. DEN: _____

10. ANC: _____

Those were easy by design, just to get you into the game. Now let's try a few destinations in the U.S. just below "major" status. (Answers on page 51, but no peeking is allowed until you've filled in the blanks):

11. AOO: _____

12. AZO: _____

13. BGR: _____

14. CLT: _____

15. FLL: _____

Now while you're checking the correct answers to those five, here are five more—this time from foreign airports of call:

16. AMS: _____

17. BKK: _____

18. BRU: _____

19. CAI: _____

20. CPH: _____

Having negotiated our way through the warmups and the first two quarters of the game, let's try our hand at putting together a story line with the airport code names. Here goes:

> *After greeting everyone at the table with a*
> *pleasant ALO, the BOS began the meeting*

with a terse comment about this year's sales: "BAH! Our effort so FAR," he exclaimed, "is for the BRDs. Now let's cut the CRP and do what we can to SLE like HEL!"

Around the table, everyone was quiet until BIL SPK up.

"We need HLP," he said to the BOS, "COS it's a SIN to SIT on our ASPs and FLL sorry for ourselves. The competition SUX. But here we SIT, month after month, and continue to PER like FAT cats. I say LSE swallow the BTR taste of our past failures and MKE our competitors go 'AOO' and 'OGG' over our success for a change!

"GRR. . . ."

Can you do any better? Here's your chance (for a list of codes, see Appendix IV).

_____

_____

_____

_____

_____

_____

_____

_____

_____

_____

_____

_____

_____

_____

_____

_____

_____

_____

_____

_____

The Correct Answers to Quiz on Page 48-49:

1. ORD = O'HARE, CHICAGO
2. ATL = ATLANTA
3. DTW = DETROIT METROPOLITAN
4. LGA = LA GUARDIA, NEW YORK
5. LAX = LOS ANGELES INTERNATIONAL
6. SLC = SALT LAKE CITY
7. WAS = WASHINGTON, D.C.
8. EWR = NEWARK, N.J.
9. DEN = DENVER
10. ANC = ANCHORAGE, ALASKA
11. AOO = ALTOONA, PA.
12. AZO = KALAMAZOO, MI.
13. BGR = BANGOR, ME.
14. CLT = CHARLOTTE, N.C.
15. FLL = FT. LAUDERDALE, FLA.
16. AMS = AMSTERDAM, HOLLAND
17. BKK = BANGKOK, THAILAND
18. BRU = BRUSSELS, BELGIUM
19. CAI = CAIRO, EGYPT
20. CPH = COPENHAGEN, DENMARK

Here's how our story would have read if we had substituted the city instead of the airport code:

After greeting everyone at the table with a pleasant Waterloo (Iowa) the Boston began the meeting with a terse comment about this year's sales: "Bahrain! Our effort so Fargo (North Dakota)" he exclaimed, "Is for the Brainerd (Minnesota). Now let's cut the Corpus Christi (Texas) and do what we can to Seoul, Korea like Helsinki, Finland."

Around the table, everyone was quiet until Billings (Montana) Sapporo, Japan up. "We need Jakarta, Indonesia," he said to the Boston, "Colorado Springs it's a Singapore to Sitka (Alaska) on our Alice Springs, Austria and Ft. Lauderdale sorry for ourselves. The competition Sioux City (Iowa). But here we Sitka and Perth, Australia like Fresno (California) cats. I say La Crosse (Wisconsin) swallow the Baton Rouge (Louisiana) taste of the past and Milwaukee our <u>competitors</u> go Altoona (Pennsylvania) and Maui (Hawaii) over <u>our</u> success! Grand Rapids (Michigan). . .

There were a total of 27 codes used in the story. How many did you guess correctly? Write the number here: _____.

7.

The World On Wheels

Be near me when my light is low,
When the blood creeps, and the nerves
prick
And tingle; and the heart is sick,
And all the wheels of Being slow.

— Alfred Lord Tennyson

$\longleftarrow$ The expression "let's not re-invent the wheel" is used countless times every day in business, as a popular admonition that history and experience shouldn't be forgotten when plans are developed for future implementation. But over the past decade, the wheel *has* been virtually reinvented as a newly-discovered means of easing the burden of travelers, enabling millions of us to enjoy greater mobility while in transit.

I'm referring, of course, to the expanding application of wheels to any and every kind of luggage bag, from hefty duffles to hanging three-suiters. Once the exclusive status symbol of flight crews, as they scurried through airports from gate to gate, the wheeled luggage bag has become a common sight among everyday traveling folks like you and me—and is a particularly helpful assist to senior citizens and handicapped travelers.

I learned early on that not all wheeled bags are equally useful. With all good intentions, my wife gave me a wheel-equipped carry-on luggage bag as an anniversary gift. But when I used it for the first time, I learned that the wheels were mounted too close together. As a result, the bag swerved, wobbled, and flipped over frequently, causing me to look like a clumsy, overserved lout. To save further embarrassment, I wound up carrying the bag most of the time, defeating the purpose of having wheels—and, at extra cost no less. Lesson learned: make sure the wheels are big enough and far enough apart to provide stability when in use. . .and don't drink before driving a wheelie.

The early wheeled bags were restricted to sizes that would fit in the aisles of aircraft, so that you could literally wheel your belongings from your drop-off point outside the terminal right to your seat—except for a brief interlude at the x-ray machine. But as the demand grew over the years, manufacturers have applied wheels to just about every type of carrier. My favorite is the large two-suiter that not only offers the mobility of wheels, but includes a spring-loaded strap on the pull-out handle that enables you to suspend other, smaller bags from the stem of the handle while you wheel your way to your terminal destination.

As the population of "wheelies" increases, you can easily discern the caste system that could be evolving in the nation's air terminals. Be on the lookout for these types, for example:

The slick, professional race driver wheelie: A luggage bag with stickers covering every inch. The wheels are wide, well-oiled, and leave a light trail of smoke as the owner speeds down the concourse. The logo decals identify

Goodyear, Pennzoil, and Midas—all desirable destinations the "driver" has visited recently, we presume.

The only-used-on-Sunday wheelie: A low-mileage bag framed in hand-made white lace, propelled at only the slowest, most patient of speeds down the concourse, never overtaking another wheelie bag headed in the same direction. The wheels are in perfect condition, sporting tiny whitewalls that are spotless at the start of every trip.

The deluxe executive suite wheelie: A bag fashioned of the finest, richest Corinthian leather, with accents of pin-striping and genuine gold-plated hardware. The wheels are covered with thick, stain-resistant carpet so they roll silently across any terminal surface. Tiny chrome wheel covers reflect the glistening of the owner's freshly-shined oxfords.

The double-shifting tandem wheelie: This one takes up half of the concourse as it comes down the aisle roaring on its overhead cam,18 heavy-duty wheels with shiny covers and chrome lug nuts. It holds enough clothing to outfit half of the state of Rhode Island and has a tendency to veer toward scales.

The Muscle-Jock Wheelie: This one rolls along with a special rhythm, so listen carefully for: "1-2-3-AND 1-2-3-AND." It has wide shoulders and a belt around the middle to keep it from bursting.

I can hardly wait for the time a wheel-equipped bag comes rolling down the baggage claim chute, careens off the circulating belt, and roars through the automatic door out to the street where six cars collide as their drivers swerve to avoid the untamed wheelie. How would you like to be holding the baggage claim for that Samsonite?

What kind of wheelies do you observe as you people-watch and wait for the next flight to your intended destination? ____

_____

_____

_____

_____

_____

_____

Post-Script: Will the next generation of air travelers feature *passengers* on wheels, roller-blading through airports with their wheelie bags trailing behind?

8.

Let's Get That Clear

The Meaning Doesn't Matter if it's only
idle chatter of a transcendental kind.
— Sir Humphrey Gilbert

W hen you're on a trip, it's important to be tuned into the latest travel lingo, so that you can communicate with gate agents, airline crew, and other passengers. For example:

The ticket agent says he's going to *waitlist* you. Is he going to:

a. List your weight on the TV monitor along with flight information?

b. Wait until he finds a list with your name on it?

c. Put you on standby for the next flight?

The flight attendant announces that it's time for *food service*. Is she going to:

a. Treat the food with a little lube oil and a dab of grease?

b. Introduce the newly-inducted men of the All Chef's Corps?

c. Try to serve dinner while everyone is in the bathroom and in the aisles?

Back to the gate agent one more time. He says he's going to *pre-board* **families with small children and elderly passengers who need extra time. Is he really preparing to:**

a. Get someone's full attention by swatting them in the head with a 2 x 4?

b. Move in with one or more of the families or senior citizens?

c. Help passengers who need special assistance to get settled on board the plane?

The pilot announces that your plane is waiting on the *tarmac.* **Are you:**

a. Expecting the arrival of a *Tonight Show* character who divines the answers, never having seen the questions that were stored in a mayonnaise jar?

b. Standing on a giant hamburger covered with secret sauce and fresh, hot tar?

c. Temporarily assigned to a holding area awaiting assignment to a runway for takeoff?

What are the special air travel words or terms—in other words, the airline "lingo" words—that puzzle you the most? Take a moment to jot down a few and make up your own definitions:

Word or Term   **Definition**

_____   _____

_____   _____

_____   _____

_____   _____

_____   _____

_____   _____

9.

The Rutabaga Phenomenon

Hence! home, you idle creatures, get you
home:
Is this a holiday?

— William Shakespeare

$\textbf{I}$'ve come to the conclusion, after exhaustive study and fastidious observation, that the world population of rutabagas is increasing at an alarming rate. And some airport terminals can be fertile breeding grounds for the irritating critters.

You've undoubtedly met a rutabaga or two yourself on your last trip—perhaps without taking special notice—but they're out there, creating customer dissatisfaction and fouling up passengers' timetables.

I've got to admit, early on, that most of the service people I've met in airport stores and restaurants are genuinely interested in handling your needs and getting you on your way promptly. But there are always exceptions.

You know a rutabaga when you see one. The record shop

clerk who mutters an almost unintelligible "Huh?" when you ask for a title that's even slightly below this week's Top 40 list, or the gum-snapping, ring-on-the-ear, cool dudes who dawdle at the opposite end of the store, hoping you'll go away without having to act on the obligation of actually "serving" you, the customer. You'll also recall a rutabaga or two who spent ten minutes of *your* time on the phone muttering sweet nothings into her boyfriend's ear while you waited to check out and pay for your travel-size bottle of Pepto Bismol®.

Rutabagas are sometimes known for their *inaction*—and, at other times, they respond rudely and carelessly when you ask the simplest of questions. They range in age generally from 18 to 25, but I once encountered a 60-something rutabaga at a discount store outlet in northern Michigan who whined openly about a delay in her break time because of the long line of customers at her register. The customers were obviously an unnerving distraction to this employee, who apparently had the distinct impression that her number one job priority was to sip Diet Coke® and munch on Doritos® to fill in her workday. Customers? Heck, they were someone else's problem.

The rutabagas who haunt airline terminals are an especially troublesome lot. At some departure areas, a few of them man the carry-on x-ray belts where they're exposed to thousands of customers hurrying to catch their flights each day. They gaze hypnotically—silently—at the x-ray screen, then suddenly bellow *"Empty your pockets!"* in a tone that would lead any passerby to believe you're hiding a nuclear warhead in your Levi's®. The opposite type lurks behind the counter of some coffee shops, where their actions reinforce their belief that you have suddenly transformed yourself into an invisible being. (Until it's time to pick up the tip, that is).

I'm seriously thinking of joining the local chapter of Stamp Out Rutabagas, International (S.O.R.I.) to rid the world of these pesky creatures and dispatch them to permanent unemployment —where they'll spend at least one day each week in line at Rutabaga Central, the nearest Federal Government Employment office, headquarters of major league-level rutabagas who inhabit the "service" counters.

Once the rutabagas are all gone, we'll replace them with— what else?—a fresh crop of **peaches**. . . with maybe a tomato or two for visual gratification. Then all will be well in the world of customer service in your favorite airline terminal.

*   *   *

Where have you encountered rutabagas today? _____

_____

_____

_____

_____

_____

Were they male or female? _____Approx. age: _____

What did they do to qualify as rutabagas? _____

_____

_____

_____

_____

10.

A Way With Words

I fear those big words, Stephen said,
which make us so unhappy.

— James Joyce

If you're just starting a business career or are already climbing the ladder, you're going to have to equip your mind with all of the proper buzz words that make business communications so obscure and complex. This chapter is designed to help you know, recognize, and understand all of the right words. It's up to you to put 'em in the right places.

Because our plan since Chapter One has been to use this waiting time productively, let's see what we can do in the next few minutes with our vocabulary (vō-'ka-bū-ler-ē: all the words of a language). And, since I don't expect that you've been lugging your *Funk and Wagnall's* all the way from Walla Walla, here are a few words I find frequently used, but also frequently misunderstood, in the world of business. See how many you can define before you look up the answers, provided through the courtesy of the *American Heritage Dictionary*:

Word   **Definition**

TANTAMOUNT: _____

SPECIOUS: _____

UBIQUITOUS: _____

COPACETIC: _____

DEMAGOGUE: _____

FACETIOUS: _____

ANOMALY: _____

QUINTESSENTIAL: _____

EPITOME: _____

ARGUABLY: _____

DEMOGRAPHIC: _____

REDUNDANT: _____

MODICUM: _____

CAPRICIOUS: _____

VILIFY: _____

ERUDITE: _____

CASTIGATE: _____

EBULLIENT: _____

STRATIFY: _____

CLICHE: _____

Before you check your definitions with the answers, make up a five sentence paragraph, using at least three of the words listed above in each of the sentences. Here goes: _____

_____

_____

_____

_____

_____

_____

Did you use the words correctly? Check it out:

TANTAMOUNT: Equivalent in effect or value.

SPECIOUS: Having the ring of truth, but actually fallacious; deceptively attractive.

UBIQUITOUS: Being or seeming to be everywhere at the same time.

COPACETIC: Excellent; first rate.

DEMAGOGUE: A leader who attains power by appealing to the emotions and prejudices of the populace.

FACETIOUS: Playfully jocular; humorous.

ANOMALY: Deviation or departure from the normal.

QUINTESSENTIAL: Being the most typical.

EPITOME: A representative or example of a class or type.

ARGUABLY: Open to argument; that can be argued plausibly.

DEMOGRAPHICS: The characteristics of human populations and population segments; used in marketing analyses to identify market segments.

REDUNDANT: Needlessly repetitive; verbose.

MODICUM: A small, moderate, or token amount.

CAPRICIOUS: Impulsive and unpredictable.

VILIFY: To make vicious and defamatory statements about.

ERUDITE: Learned.

CASTIGATE: To criticize severely.

EBULLIENT: Zestfully enthusiastic.

STRATIFY: To arrange or separate into castes, classes, or graded status levels.

CLICHE: A trite or overused expression or idea.

Because we always give 110%, we never wind up the whole ball of wax like this with something as arguably uncool and unsophistocated as a cliche, man. I mean, y'know, for real, it's just not kosher!

Note #1: crossword puzzle fans, English majors, and cheaters should have had few problems with these definitions.

Note #2: sometimes English majors and cheaters are synonymous: "having the same or similar meaning."

11.

Will It Be Cash
Or Credit Card?

*Ah, make the most of what we yet may
spend,
Before we too into the dust descend.*
                                    — Edmund Fitzgerald

✈ **I**f you get tired of listening to
14 simultaneous cellular phone conversations while you're waiting in the gate area, and you need to get up and move around,
you might want to accomplish some serious shopping or strolling, since you have plenty of time and are in a relaxed mood.
Airport shops are good sources for interesting and unusual gifts
for friends and family of all ages. . . particularly kids.

Foreign airports provide the best choices for shopping, since
they offer duty free shops that carry a broad variety of selections—often at bargain prices. You'll have to deal with the cal-
culation of currency exchange rates, but it's a minor inconve-
nience when you have so much fascinating merchandise to
choose from. And, there's an added benefit: they'll often deliver your purchases to the plane.

In the United States, my two choices for best airport shopping facilities are in Pittsburgh and Minneapolis. The Pittsburgh terminal, built in the eighties, is comfortable, well-designed, and focused around a central **AIRMALL** of 60-plus stores stocking everything from autographed sports memorabilia to name-brand clothing, art prints, and gourmet coffees and teas. It even boasts of its own postal store.

A well-known Calder mobile, titled "Pittsburgh," is suspended over the retail mall, having been relocated from the Carnegie Museum where it was displayed since 1979.

One of the benefits of airport shopping is the availability of local team apparel. Therefore, if your son or daughter would go bonkers over a Pittsburgh Penguin team jersey or a baseball cap with a Steeler logo, now's your chance to stock up. . . while supplies last.

Here are my Top 40 Airports for travelers to be stranded in, in case your current or future itinerary calls for a long layover, unexpected delay, or flight cancellation:

40: Chicago Midway

39: Austin, Texas

38: Montreal, Quebec

37: Traverse City, Michigan

36: Toronto, Ontario

35: New York Kennedy

34: Boston

33: San Diego

32: Philadelphia

31: Grand Rapids, Michigan

30: St. Louis

29: Detroit

28: Columbus, Ohio

27: Washington National

26: Cleveland

25: San Francisco

24: Washington Dulles

23: New York La Guardia

22: Ft. Lauderdale

21: Milwaukee

20: Kansas City

19: Phoenix

18: Lansing, Michigan

17: Ft. Myers, Fla.

16: Los Angeles

15: Tampa

14: Jacksonville

13: Houston International

12: Orlando

11: Long Beach John Wayne

NUMBER 10: PORTLAND

Oregon Marketplace, in the Portland main terminal, includes stores like Made in Oregon, where you can find (and buy) local favorites, including marionberry and huckleberry preserves, hand-crafted souvenirs, Tillamook cheese, and Pendleton wool apparel. And, to protect yourself against the rainy Oregon weather, you may consider investing in the Oregon Headroof, a large-brimmed fisherman's-type hat that can be easily stowed in your bag until your next trip to the Pacific Northwest. (That's assuming you ever get a chance to sample the weather outside of the Portland air terminal.)

NUMBER 9: BALTIMORE

You might be tempted to treat your palate to dehydrated astronaut food at the Baltimore-Washington International Airport—anything's better than most airline dinners—but plan to spend as much time as possible checking out the hundreds of other interesting offerings at the terminal's Smithsonian Air and Space Museum store. There you can find defunct airlines' (like Eastern, Pan Am, and Piedmont) metal logos and "wings" for your son or daughter. Model airplanes, aviation-related jewelry, Blue Angel videos, and a model Space Shuttle are some of the other unique "take-homers" you'll want to slip into your carry-on bag (after you pay for them, of course).

The Smithsonian shop is a feature of the Observation Gallery, aviation-theme displays that offer interactive participation. You and your traveling companions can settle into the cockpit of a Boeing 737, eavesdrop on air traffic control transmissions, and review weather maps of the destination city to which you hope to eventually fly.

But back down on earth, be sure to look up a seafood restaurant serving Chesapeake Bay crab or crab cakes before you leave. A local specialty, crab is to Baltimore what lobster is to Boston. Don't miss the taste-testing opportunity while you're in the waiting mode.

NUMBER 8: ATLANTA

At Hartsfield International airport, a new four-level mall of shops was opened recently in the main terminal. More than 225,000 square feet of space is devoted to goods and services offered to transient consumers.

The international Concourse E welcomes foreign visitors with an extraordinary showcase of contemporary art and architecture that features bright colors, arched skylights, artistic light fixtures, strong building design forms, and flowing spaces.

NUMBER 7: DALLAS

Since Texans like to do things in extraordinary proportions, facilities for shopping at the Dallas-Ft. Worth International airport have been expanded to provide over 50 retail shops and more than 100 food and beverage outlets—not to mention a selection of free-standing kiosks. And "street pricing" policies are enforced, ensuring that the prices of restaurant meals are comparable with other Dallas locations.

The airport terminal here is a great place to stock up on Dallas Cowboys wearing apparel and souvenirs. You can't go

wrong when you display your allegiance to "America's Team," can you? Or, if you hanker for some unique vittles, pardner, try these airport shop specialties:

▲ "Armadillo Droppings" (chocolate candy)
▲ "Hot Buckshot" (salsa made from black beans)
▲ "Texas Champagne" (hot sauce that will set your stomach on fire)

The Dallas-Ft. Worth airport was the world's fourth busiest in 1995, offering its facilities to 54.4 million passengers, or 150,000 on average per day.

According to the airport's director of commercial development, management philosophy is to "make the airport exciting and entertaining so that people who fly through DFW will make a conscious decision to come back through Dallas the next time they make flight reservations." With the changes and improvements underway, they just might.

NUMBER 6: CINCINNATI

Finding a mate (Chapter 3) isn't the only interesting pastime you can become engaged in at the Greater Cincinnati/Northern Kentucky airport in Covington. . . though it's certainly a unique way in which to cope with a flight delay or cancellation.

If you're not in the mood for mate-hunting, there are always the Queen City Country Store outlets (five in all) to soak up your time and your dollars. You could, for example, pick up a supply of ointment originally designed to help dairy farmers soften up cow's udders. The concoction, now commercially known as Bag Balm, is the best choice for soothing problems with dry, chapped hands.

Some of the other down-home products at Queen City Country Store include: Raggedy Ann dolls, bread and butter pickles, and sidewalk chalk (think of the warm welcome you'll get when little Susie and Johnnie find out you've brought them a gross of sidewalk chalk from Kentucky!).

NUMBER 5: MINNEAPOLIS

Actually, the best feature of the Minneapolis airport isn't at the airport, but in nearby Bloomington, at the $650 million Mall of America. There's plenty of comfortable transportation available to take you to and from this shoppers' paradise, which is a short van ride from the terminal door. Mall of America also includes a sprawling, contemporary amusement park, with lots of ways to tire out the kids. It's all indoors, so you won't be affected by one of Minneapolis' frequent winter snow storms.

Attractions of the Mall include "UnderWater World," a 1.2 million gallon walk-through aquarium with over 8,000 fish, amphibians, and reptiles; Knott's Camp Snoopy, the largest indoor family theme park in the U.S.—seven acres of rides and entertainment venues; and the LEGO® Imagination Center — which includes 30 giant models built totally out of LEGO bricks. The models include space shuttles, dinosaurs, and the world's largest interactive and musical clock tower.

More visitors flow through the Mall of America annually than Disney World and the Grand Canyon combined, even though it is relatively new—having opened in '92.

It's also large enough to house 32 Boeing 747s within its interior.

Back at the Lindbergh terminal of the Minneapolis/St. Paul International airport, the new central concession area has been rebuilt in a "boulevard" format featuring more than a dozen gift and food shops. The airport terminal is well laid out and offers many amenities to the transient passenger—but that Mall of America seems mighty tempting to the traveler who has two hours or more to kill.

NUMBER 4: LAS VEGAS

If you have to be stranded anywhere in the U.S., Las Vegas is **the** place for raw entertainment, when you tire of watching the departure monitors. Known for providing endless opportunities to overindulge, Vegas gives you every possible chance to partake in games of chance—even at the airport. You'll find slot machines and other gambling opportunities in even the most remote nook and cranny of the Las Vegas airport terminal, offering more than a handful of ways for you to hand over your loose coins and possibly scoop up a few along the way. If you tire of gambling or your supply of coins runs out, you can shop for a variety of tacky western goods and miniature gambling paraphernalia that can make you a loser on your home turf.

One of my favorite memories of Las Vegas was attending Mass one Sunday morning at a Catholic church just off the infamous "strip." After a stirring homily, the presiding priest paused to point out that the Sunday collection was about to begin, and that tokens, chips and checks would be gratefully accepted — as well as plain old cold cash, of course. "We're not fussy about the form of your contribution," he instructed the congregation. "We'll be inspired to find a way to cash it in."

NUMBER 3: PITTSBURGH

Its central mall is a stunning discovery for first-time visitors to the airport in Steel City. Shaped like an "X," the mall serves as a crossover point for just about everyone who's coming and going.

The 60-plus modern, pleasant stores that make up the mall are top-notch consumer choices that provide a wide variety of merchandise—from an autographed picture of Mean Joe Green to the latest in airline memorabilia. When you're hungry, you can stop for a meal in one of over 20 restaurant choices, including one (are you ready for this?) called Wok and Roll, to stoke up for the remainder of your journey.

NUMBER 2: ANY ONE OF THESE WILL DO

If you can't choose to be delayed at the Vegas or Pittsburgh airports, try being cancelled in Seattle. There, to help you cope with the feeling of isolation and anxiety that naturally over-whelms a stranded air traveler, is a bank of comfortable "ergo-nomically correct" easy chairs and a squad of masseuses and masseurs on duty to soothe your nerves with a 15-minute mas-sage for $13.00 or a "double dose" for $22.00. Once you expe-rience the therapeutic effect of their nimble hand exercises, you might find yourself actually *hoping* to be stranded in Seattle (especially at the entrance to Concourse C, where the Massage Bar is located).

(A welcome, recent addition to New York's Kennedy Air-port is the Great American Backrub Store, located in the depar-ture area of the International Arrivals building. For instant ten-sion relief, you can enjoy a five-minute massage for $8.95 or splurge and get a 20-minute massage for $24.95).

When in Palm Springs, do as the natives do while waiting at the airport: step outside near gates 4 and 5 and enjoy access to a sizeable putting green with golf balls and putters furnished to travelers in need of relaxation. And in Miami, between Con-courses C and D, you could visit the "meditation room" that is equipped with 20 blue easy chairs, a couple of oak tables, a palm tree, and a Monet print on the wall—all designed to calm your nerves and energize your spirit.

There are no Monet prints at the country's newest airport, a $4.2 billion facility in Denver, but the spectacular vistas of the snow-covered Rocky Mountains through the terminal's sweep-ing glass windows are almost worth the waiting. And, if you tire of the view, spend a few moments gazing at the works of over 40 artists on display as part of a $7.5 million permanent public art collection exhibited in the new airport terminal. And, if you're inspired to spend money, a generous potpourri of contemporary shops offer the latest selections of apparel, gift items, and souvenirs.

If you're traveling overseas and find your flight cancelled or delayed, try hoping that you're in Amsterdam's Schiphol airport, rated by England's *Business Traveller* magazine as the best European airport for **11 consecutive years**. There you'll not only find minor gambling devices like 75 slots, but a full casino with a roulette wheel and three black jack tables to lighten your billfold. This facility has the distinction of being the world's only casino with a clock, so that patrons can make their flights on time.

A recently-added feature is high-tech golf, which enables you to play a simulated round "at" 26 top courses around the world. Golf pros are on duty to offer lessons, and you can practice on the putting green while you wait.

The nearby Sun Centre Schiphol features exercise machines, tanning booths, and massage tables. Showers are available for about $10.00.

If you're stranded in any airport, you need to do everything you can to avoid "gatelock." A recent article in *The Wall Street Journal* describes the term as "the traveler's tendency to rush to the departure gate, nab a seat, and then—as if paralyzed— homestead in place."

Cross "homesteading" off your list of things to do while waiting in an airport. You've got more to accomplish with your life than spend any more of it than necessary in an airport departure lounge.

12.

O'Hare
The Winner—Flaps Down

There's always room at the top.
— Daniel Webster

✈ **I**f you happen to be hung up at O'Hare in Chicago, you probably don't care that you find yourself in a town known, at various times, as "Gangster Land," "Hog Butcher," "Windy City," and "Second City." But Chicago's a great town to explore if you have the time. And if your flight's been cancelled, you probably have the time.

O'Hare is in a category by itself as a place to spend "idle" time, simply because it's so huge and offers so many different, beneficial facilities to transient travelers and their families. And while it is large, the airport has sensible and convenient ground transportation to get you where you need to go.

For example, a train is available near the terminal to transport you to downtown Chicago in less than 30 minutes. Once there, you can discover an interesting blend of attractions, from world-renowned museums to one of the newest and largest "Planet Hollywood" restaurants. It's also the location of some

of the world's finest stores and boutiques, particularly along
Michigan Avenue.

> Rail service into the downtown area is available from
> airports in Chicago, Cleveland, Atlanta, Boston,
> Oakland, Philadelphia, and Washington, D.C. The
> cost per trip ranges from about a dollar in Boston
> to just over $4.00 in Philly.

But if you prefer to stay at the O'Hare terminals, there's
still plenty to do to help pass the time in an interesting way.
Take a walk to either of the United terminal wings and experience the unique light show in the lower-level tunnel connecting
the twin United concourses. Designed by Michael Hayden, an
internationally-known artist, the neon sculpture runs the length
of the tunnel ceiling. The kinetic piece is composed of neon
light tubes programmed to provide continuously changing light
patterns, accompanied by recorded music ("Rhapsody in Blue,"
no less) you can hear throughout the length of the tunnel. Kids,
particularly, will find it an eye-arresting experience they'll remember for a long time.

The United terminal is designed to resemble a nineteenth
century railroad station, with glass skylights, reminiscent of classic structures like the Galleria of Milan, Italy. There's enough
glass in these ceilings to dome both Wrigley Field and Comiskey
Park, favorite haunts of Chicago baseball fans.

For contrast, stroll over to the non-denominational chapel
on the Mezzanine level of Terminal 2 for a few moments of
quiet, contemplative time. Ministers and priests take turns in
offering services at various times, particularly on weekends. (You

may want to say an extra prayer for the mechanics who are work-ing to get your flight airborne eventually).

O'Hare has an automated computer-controlled rail system that connects the terminals, so you can navigate from one end of the airport to the other quickly and conveniently. . . even with bags in hand. The Automated Transit System runs from the long-term parking lot through five stops to Terminal 1. The 2.9 mile trip takes approximately 7-1/2 minutes.

If traversing the concourses is more to your liking, you'll probably build a healthy appetite. To satisfy your hunger, some O'Hare concessionaires offer custom-made low-fat sandwiches, salads and fresh fruit selections for the fitness-conscious. They also provide special packaging that will enable you to carry sand-wiches and beverages on board your departing flight. Or, you can find more unique choices in the ethnic food mall in Con-course C.

O'Hare offers a potpourri of amenities for the benefit of the delayed passenger. For example, the O'Hare Stranded Pas-senger program provides cots, blankets, pillows, and travel kits when flights are delayed or cancelled by weather. And, they set aside designated areas where passengers can catch a few ZZZZZZZZs before heading out to their gates in the morning.

There are reading/quiet areas surrounded by live trees. And, to demonstrate the range of their concern for travelers, O'Hare is the only airport I know of that provides plastic covers for every toilet seat. You press a button and the gadget automati-cally rotates the plastic to give you a fresh covering.

In the new International terminal, one of the most irritating challenges—finding local currency to rent a baggage cart upon arrival—is solved at O'Hare. Carts are provided free of charge.

And, they can be used through the Customs area and up to the baggage check-in desks for domestic flight connections, where baggage can be placed on a conveyor belt and sent to your next flight.

Once free of baggage, arriving international flight passengers get to admire floor-to-ceiling montages depicting scenes of famous landmarks and neighborhoods around Chicago. And, there are painted murals offering international artists' interpretations of the city.

O'Hare serves over 67 million passengers each year, averaging over 100 aircraft arriving or departing each hour. About 175,000 passengers pass through the airport on any given day.

Serving the needs of that many people requires many amenities and offerings. And you get to take advantage of all these benefits while you wait for your flight to board at this, the classiest of U.S. airports, and the world champion in passenger traffic.

WORLD'S BUSIEST AIRPORTS IN 1995

Chicago O'Hare: 67.3 million passengers
Atlanta Hartsfield: 57.7 million
London Heathrow: 54.5 million
Dallas-Ft. Worth: 54.4 million
L.A. International: 53.9 million

13.

Walking On Fingertips

Well, if I called the wrong number,
why did you answer the phone?

— James Thurber

✈ One common feature of all airport terminals is the availability of phones in multiple locations. And, since your legs are probably tired from the shopping experiences you enjoyed in Chapter 11, it may be a good idea to "sit a spell" while you "take a load off" your feet. But you don't have to halt your shopping expedition. Why not shop by phone?

If you have access to an airline club lounge, you'll find it an ideal place to do some phone shopping during your flight delay. Here are some of the goods and services you can access easily, without running up your phone card bill:

CREDI-CALL: 800-364-7933, Ext. 8600
Start by buying some phone time. A new service called Credi-Call will sell you an hour and 45 minutes of calling time at the

low cost of $25.00. You can use the service to call anywhere in the USA any time of the day or night. And, if your card is stolen and used, you're responsible only for the $25.00 max.

1-800-FLOWERS

Now that you have the time, you can make someone happy by sending flowers for an upcoming special occasion, as an expression of appreciation to your clients, or to congratulate an associate on a special accomplishment. Satisfaction is guaranteed.

Headquartered in Westbury, Long Island, New York, this organization handles phone orders 24 hours a day for beautiful floral bouquets delivered anywhere in the world. You can also call them to have a variety of specialty items delivered, including gift baskets and balloons.

If you ask for their Flower of the Month program, you'll be able to enroll in a reminder service that will make sure you are notified when a birthday, anniversary, or other special occasion is coming up among your family, friends, and business acquaintenances. It's a great idea for business people who like to express birthday and anniversary greetings to associates and clients. The reminder service, provided without charge, beats walking around all year with a string around your finger.

1-800-FLOWERS can be contacted by phone or through online services from your computer 365 days a year.

AUDIO BOOK CLUB: 800-422-2258

You can save up to $90 off publisher's price when you buy four audio book tapes for 99 cents. Select from a significant library of classics and current best-sellers.

STAIR MASTER: 800-STAIR 99

You can order a stair-stepping machine for your home. Aerobic workouts can improve your mental and physical well-being. Video and catalog available.

TRANSMEDIA: 800-806-DINE

Earn frequent flyer miles every time you dine and show your Transmedia network card at over 5,800 restaurants nationwide. You'll be credited with ten times each dollar spent in the selected TM establishments ($50.00 in dining charges = 500 miles earned).

SOUNDVIEW: 800-521-1227

Instead of letting business books pile up on your credenza, because you're too busy to read an entire book, read Soundview

Executive Book Summaries to get the core content without investing a lot of time.

SYBERVISION: 800-678-0777

Order All-Audio language cassettes to learn a foreign language —and get a free Sony® Walkman to help you play the tapes.

KORDENE PUBLICATIONS: 800-879-4214

Get another copy or two of this book for friends and fellow travelers. Ask for *Holding Pattern, Volume I.* (There's no Volume II, but who knows?)

INFORMATION

To find out the toll-free number of any business or individual listing, call 800-555-1212.

Of course, if you have a laptop or notebook computer, along with a modem, you could do all of your shopping by going online. "The Marketplace" on America Online®, and similar shopping centers on other online services, provides a convenient means of selecting the goods you want without even leaving your chair, although some purchases require a toll-free call to present your credit card information.

In any event, surfing and shopping are certainly improvements in your use of airport waiting time—instead of staring into outer space or putting on calories—unless, of course, you're munching on donut holes while you punch your laptop.

14.

People-Watching
Can Be Educational

What kind of people do they
think we are?

— Winston Churchill

In small towns or large cities, the airport terminal is one of the greatest places to people-watch. In Las Vegas, for example, you'll see a few winners, many losers, and probably a celebrity or two arriving or departing. There's a lot of convention business there, so you'll encounter hordes of transient members of every imaginable organization, from the National Home Builders to the Beautiful Body Builders.

If you look carefully, you're likely to discover these species flying to or from their nests through the Las Vegas airport at all hours of the day and night:

▲ The *Blue-Haired, Midwestern, Crackle-Voiced Granny* who clutches her souvenir slot machine coin bucket, and can be identified instantly by her empty pockets.

- ▲ The *Big-Bellied, Bleary-Eyed, Beersucking Loudmouth,* whose presence is known by the blare of his rapturous mating call: "Hey, turkeys, where are dem broads?"

- ▲ The *Tee-Shirted, Bloodshot-Eyed Black Jack,* who whistles under his breath and keeps muttering, "hit me. . . hit me. . . hit me" at least a hundred times during his walk down the long concourse.

- ▲ The *Big-Breasted, Mink-Feathered, High-Heeled Warbler,* who is on her flight to stardom, escorted on this leg of the journey by a *Wide-Lapeled, Cigar-Chewing, Sunglassed, Pock-Skinned Predator* who steers her every move by a firm clutch of her arm.

You'll identify dozens of interesting species during even a short stay at McCarran Airport in Las Vegas—and you won't need binoculars.

Maybe you'll find birds of a completely different flock in your airport.

Try identifying and describing the most interesting species:

1. _____

2. _____

3. _____

4. _____

5. _____

*   *   *

In my experience, many of the people who walk the terminal concourses each day are local residents whose dress frequently sets them apart from transient tourists.

In the Denver airport, watch for boots as the prevailing symbol of the area. In Dallas, it's 10-gallon hats. In California, bright shirts, tanned skin and sunglasses. In Florida, locals wear white shoes and "snowbirds" carry netted bags of oranges or grapefruits. In Chicago, one of the most common sights is shopping bags from the Minneapolis Mall of America. If you're in Boston, look for the lobster carriers. In Milwaukee, many of the locals sport Green Bay Packer sweatshirts. In Detroit, it's University of Michigan shirts or Piston jackets and Detroit Tiger caps. Visitors to San Francisco can be identified by the sourdough bread bags they cling to while on the move.

What are the prevailing themes symbolizing your fellow travelers in the airport where you're stranded? _____

_____

_____

_____

15.

Get Fit, Not Fat

*Has it ever struck you that there's
a thin man inside every
fat man, just as they say there's a
statue inside every block of stone?*

— George Orwell

The initial temptation is to visit the terminal doughnut shop and eat your way through the idle hours—or drown them away with six or seven beers. But that's not what was intended by the phrase "Travel can be broadening." Even if you're "into fitness," it may benefit you to think about these "lookouts":

1. Frequent flying can penalize your body if you lose your discipline, drink liquor, eat fatty foods, and don't maintain an exercise regimen.

2. Dehydration can have a major effect on your body during and after a long trip. The humidity level on board most airliners ranges as low as 8%, and even lower on lengthy flights. You will need to compensate for the dry conditions by drinking lots of fresh water—and no alcohol—before, during, and after your flight.

91

3. On long trips, jet lag, lack of sleep, lack of exercise, stress, separation, and irregular consumption of pre-scription medications will complicate your life.

    To counter these negatives, here are just a few of the simple preparations you can do while waiting for your flight.

    ▲   Use the long terminal concourses as a walking track for exercise that will leave you fresh and invigo-rated; there are also a lot of interesting people and shop windows to look at along the way;

    ▲   Check out the availability of exercise rooms with stationary bikes and rowing machines;

    ▲   Walk over to the airport hotel to investigate their facilities for fitness exercise, future meeting accom-modations, or rates for an overnight stay;

    ▲   See how many times you can climb the terminal stairway within 15 minutes of vigorous exercise.

If you're marooned at LAX Airport in Los Angeles, con-sider hobbling over to the nearby Skytel where you'll find a shower and a waiting/rest area you can use after a stimulating fitness walk in the airport.

In most terminals, concourses were made for walking. So why not take advantage of the open space while you're waiting? Find the concourse with the least traffic and take off in your comfortable, well-fitting walking shoes.

If you don't want to stray too far from your gate area, find the nearest movable sidewalk—hopefully, unoccupied—and get on facing against the direction of the belt. *Eureka*: You've just created your own simulated treadmill! Do the same on an unpopulated escalator and you will have invented your own "stair-stepper."

In the heart of Texas, hustle your tired doggies on over to the Hyatt Regency hotel, adjacent to the Dallas-Ft. Worth Airport, and you'll find a first-class fitness facility—available at a guest pass rate of only $5.00—where you can enjoy a pool, exercise gear, a sauna, and a steam room.

Back at O'Hare in Chicago, you can work out the kinks in an 8,000-square-foot health club located in the Airport Hilton, which is connected by tunnel to the O'Hare terminals. For $12.00, you can spend up to four hours toning, running a treadmill marathon, perspiring in the sauna, or swinging a golf club in a simulator booth.

Maybe your time is limited to the interval between gates. If they're a considerable distance apart, approach the walk as an opportunity to work out before you fold yourself into yet another pretzel position on board your next flight.

Between-flight fitness can be fun. And it can help you live longer. Go for it!

Remember these easy-to-perform tips:

▲ Travel light and dress to be comfortable, but not sloppy.

▲ Pack or wear a good pair of walking shoes and use them often during your trip.

▲ Order special low-fat and low-sodium meals in advance of your flight date (check with your airline to determine the deadline for ordering).

▲ Don't eat the nuts served on board — they'll provide you with little hunger-satisfaction and lots of
   fat calories.

▲ Drink plenty of water and carry your own bottled
   water on board if possible.

▲ Equip yourself with an inflatable neck-rest so you
   can get some nap time without acquiring a case of
   the head-bobs or neck-twisters.

▲ When you're not napping, get up and walk around
   frequently. Get your blood moving and loosen up
   your joints every hour or so. But don't trip over a
   food cart and spill the noodles with gravy on the
   Armani suit of the guy behind you, or you may find
   yourself setting a new record for the 747 sprint. Of
   all the parts of your body to exercise on your flight,
   use your brain most frequently.

16.

Smiling Is Good For Your Health

Better by far you should forget and smile
Than that you should remember and be
*   sad.*
                              — Christina Rossetti

$\not\leftarrow$ Studies have shown that laughter is among the best natural antidotes in times of stress. So, instead of making yourself miserable with a bout of depression because your plane isn't whisking you away on schedule, try a few guffaws to ease your anxiety attack. Take these and call me in the morning:

> *A state patrolman observed a vehicle*
> *weaving in and out of traffic, veering from*
> *one lane to the other, causing other drivers*
> *to swerve to keep from colliding with the*
> *errant convertible. The cop turned on his*
> *siren and flashing lights and began to chase*
> *the wayward speeder, finally catching up*

with him a mile or so up the freeway. As he closed in on the target vehicle, he noticed that the driver was busily knitting a sweater while trying to maintain control of the steering wheel with his knees.

"Pull over!" the officer shouted through the loud speaker on top of his patrol car.

"No, cardigan!" the driver responded calmly.

(DRUM ROLL)

*   *   *

A guy walks into a bar with a dirty, mangy mongrel on a leash, bellies up to the bar and says, "If I can prove my dog can talk, how 'bout a free drink?"

*The bartender responds, "Buddy, I want you and that ugly mutt outta here right **now!**"*

"No, wait," the man counters. "Listen to this." He turns to the dog and says, "Jake, what's on top of this bar?"

The dog responds, "ROOF. . . ROOF!"

Bartender: "Look fella, I already told you once.

Take your dog and get lost."

"Give us another chance," the thirsty dog-owner replied. "Here, Jake. Tell the crowd who was the best player ever to don the pinstripes of the New York Yankees?"

The dog looked around, raised his snoot, and barked "RUTH . . . RUTH!"

By this time, the impatient bartender had both of them by their respective collars and ushered them violently through the door and out onto the sidewalk.

After a few uncomfortable moments, the dog sat up, turned his sad eyes toward his master and muttered, apologetically, "Should I have said DiMaggio?"

* * *

The Jethro family was embarrassed by the strange antics of Uncle Herman, who thought and pranced around like a chicken. Finally, they consulted a psychiatrist, who concluded that ol' Uncle Herman should be put away in the nearest coop—er, institution.

"Can't do that," Herman's wife, Tess, protested. "We've grown accustomed to the convenient supply of eggs every morning!"

* * *

A young athlete says to his coach: "I'd give my right arm to be ambidextrous."

* * *

Father to son: "Son, I've told you a billion times not to exaggerate!"

* * *

Plaintive songs on a country jukebox:

"I Don't Know Whether to Kill Myself. . . or Go Bowling."

"I Can Have My Cake and Edith, Too."

"Get Your Tongue Out of My Mouth, 'Cause I'm Kissin' You Goodbye"

* * *

Letter to a newspaper advice columnist:

"Dear Miss _____:

My husband is being released from the Army next week, and he has a good job lined up. We now have 2 children and would like to have another, but I read recently that every third baby born into the world is Chinese, so I'm afraid to take a chance. What do you think?

Source: Journal of Court Reporting

* * *

My (Former) Boss

I'd like to express, but I'm at a loss
For words when I try to describe my boss.
He starts each day at an early hour
And does his best to delegate power.

Our progress while he's been our chief
Has been super, much to the Board's relief.
So where, you say, is my dog-gone beef?
He's a soft-spoken man. . . and I'm a trifle "deef."

When he specifies what he wants me to do
I hear every *other* word, so I haven't a clue
He wants one thing, and I produce another.
Sometimes I act like a dumb little brother.

When he requested a foreign trip plan
I misunderstood; soon everything hit the fan.
He had spelled out the route far and near
But he spoke softly— and I failed to hear.

So suddenly I'm fired, and I won't be back
For instead of landing in London or Paris
Or his beloved, romantic Rome,
Guess who's shivering in downtown Nome?

*   *   *

Or try these limericks on your smile-meter:

> There was an old hound named Louie
> Who hankered for the taste of Chop Suey.
> But one day the mutt
> Began to act like a nut
> 'Cause the Chop Suey drove Louie screwy.

*   *   *

> There was a flight attendant named Sue
> Who always knew precisely what to do.
> On one morning's flight
> Two men began to fight
> So Sue served the two the flu.

*   *   *

Got a better one? Use your loose time to jot down a couple of limericks of your own. It's a fun exercise, and you'll probably outdo Louie and Sue in my examples above. Give it a try!

Limerick rule of rhyme: Start by rhyming the last words of the first two lines, then write two more lines that conclude with a different rhyme. Finish it off with a "punch line" that rhymes with the second line.

> There was a _____
> Who _____
> _____
> _____
> _____

Try again:

There once was a _____

Who _____

_____

_____

_____

Finally, with that bit of poetic injustice out of our systems, here are a few profound thoughts to ponder as you draw ever nearer to takeoff:

▲ Why are there interstate highways in Hawaii?

▲ Why do we drive on parkways and park on driveways?

▲ Why is it that when you transport something by car it's called a **ship**ment, and by boat it's called **car**go?

▲ If nothing sticks to Teflon®, how do they make Teflon stick to the pan?

▲ If they can make the "little black box" on airplanes indestructible in a crash, why can't they do the same for the entire plane?

▲ Why do they put braille dots on the keypad of a drive-up ATM machine?

Feeling more relaxed? Good, 'cause the next chapter will put you to work.

17.

Memoirs
Make the Mind Go Mellow

Oft, in the stilly night,
Ere Slumber's chain has bound me,
Fond Memory brings the light
Of other days around me.

— Thomas Moore

If you're still not out of your mental funk, here's another technique I have used with solid success. With your pad of paper and pencil in hand, think of happy times you have enjoyed with your family over the years. Jot down a few recollections to get the juices flowing—then expand your story with more details, expand again with even more, and soon you'll have the start of a Memory Book your kids and/or grandkids will treasure for a lifetime. Here's an example of one of my most notable family memories to help get you started:

"A Magical Moment with Merlin"

I'm just an ordinary guy who came from an average family who lived their average lives on the prosaic Polish-German south side of Milwaukee. But I've had the special experience of meeting and working with extraordinary people throughout my marketing career. One of these people was Merlin Olsen, Hall of Fame ex-football star with the Los Angeles Rams and former NBC and CBS football broadcaster.

When I was marketing director for Florists' Transworld Delivery Association (FTD) in the 1980s, we hired Merlin as our spokesman to help us market flowers in TV and radio commercials and in print media. Merlin did an excellent job for several years and actually became the *industry* spokesman over that time—even though he worked no more than 23 days for us each year. We paid him many large stacks of dollars for his effort in the 23-day period, and he gave us many millions of dollars of sales in return for that investment.

While under contract with us for our advertising program, Merlin also continued his career as Dick Enberg's partner on NBC telecasts of National Football League games each week.

Whenever he came into town to broadcast a Detroit Lions football game, he'd contact us in advance and we'd get together with him as schedules allowed. One such encounter took place at a local restaurant a couple of nights prior to the Thanksgiving game in 1984. During the conversation over dinner, Merlin asked whether any of us had planned to attend the game. I volunteered that I was bringing my three sons to the event, which was a holiday family tradition in Detroit for many years.

"Would your boys like to see how the game is broadcast in the TV booth?" he inquired.

"I'm sure they would, but I don't want you to go out of your way with all the stuff you have to be concerned about," I replied.

"Never mind," he snapped. "Here—hand them my business card at the pressbox entrance just before halftime and we'll show you and the boys how we do what we do during the game."

When we showed up for the game, all four of us were excited about the prospect of visiting the pressbox. The contest on the field was nothing but a time-consuming distraction while we patiently waited for the appropriate moment to abandon our seats for the trip upstairs. When the time finally came, we rushed up the ramp and knocked on the pressbox door. Predictably, we were intercepted by a muscular security guard.

The critical question was, "Would the business card *work*?"

No sweat. When the guard read Merlin's note and signature on the back of the card, he stepped aside and said, "Yes sir—just walk to the broadcast level and an usher will show you to the NBC booth." The process was clicking on all cylinders and in a minute or two we found ourselves standing outside the door displaying the well-known peacock logo. Merlin came out during a commercial break and said, "Hang around out here until the half, and then I'll introduce you around." He shook all the boys' hands, and I was on Cloud Nine. Dad of the Year, hands-down.

While we were waiting for the first half to end, we observed sportscaster Ahmad Rashad of NBC (former Minnesota Viking pass-catcher) being attended to by a busy makeup man. Rashad was perspiring profusely and the makeup guy kept patting his head with puffs of makeup, trying to prepare him for an on-camera appearance in a couple of minutes.

What we didn't realize at the time was that Ahmad had proposed on-air during the pre-game show on NBC to Phylicia Ayers-Allen—who was best known for her portrayal of Bill Cosby's wife (Claire Huxtable) on *The Cosby Show*. While we

waited for Merlin, Rashad was waiting impatiently for her response—which was to be broadcast from a New York studio
during the halftime break. Without all of this background information, we couldn't figure out what all the sweating was about.

At long last, the teams left the field and Merlin welcomed
us to the booth. He had us meet the director, the spotters, and
Dick Enberg, his sidekick. All of them treated us like VIPs.
Merlin said it would be okay for us to observe a few minutes of
the actual game coverage, if we slid into the back of the booth at
the start of the second half. We nodded enthusiastically.

Then he had another brilliant idea. "How about a picture
to remember this occasion?" he asked the boys. They nodded
obediently, still awed by his massive presence (he played defen-
sive tackle during his career with the Rams).

Merlin waved to the Lions' public relations coordinator, Bill Keenist and, as if by magic, he produced a camera in a matter of seconds. Orchestrating the experience, Merlin had us group around him and pose for a couple of candid shots. A few days later, an envelope arrived with prints of the photo—one of which hangs proudly in our basement recreation room.

The booth visit was one of the priceless experiences we have had as a family, and Merlin single-handedly made it happen.

P.S. Only Ahmad Rashad had a better day that Thanksgiving holiday. Phylicia accepted, and they were married a few months later.

*   *   *

Whether you've got a celebrity encounter to write about or not doesn't matter. A recollection of your lifetime experiences will be treasured by your family for generations. Why not start your Memory Book right now, while you've got nothing but time on your hands?

(Tip: Combining your story with pictures, later on, will make the end result even more valuable.)

If you have any difficulty in starting your story, try these openings:

"I remember" _____

_____

_____

_____

_____

Or, "My dad once told me. . ." _____

_____

_____

_____

_____

Or, you might start by describing an object that was important to the history of your family—a special house, a favorite vacation spot, or an unusual family heirloom, etc. _____

_____

_____

_____

_____

Another form of Memory Book is the personal journal or diary that provides the reader with a chronicle of your activities and thoughts for each day covered. What would you write about today's events and observations? _____

_____

_____

_____

_____

_____

_____

_____

_____

_____

_____

18.

Where Am I From?

Ah, did you once see Shelley plain,
And did he stop and speak to you
And did you speak to him again?
How strange it seems, and new!

—Robert Browning

$\mathbf{W}$hile you've been observing the habits of both the transient and home folks during your unplanned stay in the terminal, you've probably also overheard a dozen or more idle conversations. Have you noticed the distinctive characteristics of the speaking habits of your waiting area neighbors?

For example, if you heard someone ask, "Where's the nearest bubbler?" he or she is likely to be from Wisconsin—where "bubbler" is commonly used as another name for drinking fountain. When it was time to enjoy an ice cream bar on a warm summer night in Milwaukee, we begged our parents for a "paddle pop." Many of the Wisconsin fans pass up hot dogs at sporting events and gobble up several "brats" (bratwurst sandwiches) instead. If you're attending a game there and want to order a "brat," you'll sound a lot more like a local fan if you pronounce "brat" as if it rhymes with "mott" and not with "gnat."

If another traveler in your waiting area reported that he had "pahked his cah" at the long-term lot, you'd probably recognize he's from New England, where dogs often "bahk up the wrong tree." And if you happen to be in the real England, or even in Africa, you may hear interesting expressions like "panel beaters" to describe a car body shop. And you'll also hear some interesting modes of pronunciation.

Along with my boss and his wife, Lou and Cindy Brand, Nancy and I hired a driver in London a few years back for a trip to Cambridge, where we were to attend a business conference. When the driver showed up at our hotel, he introduced himself simply as Ray—pronounced "Rye," he emphasized. He was a great driver and pointed out many of the interesting sights along the way as we traveled up to Cambridge through a fascinating maze of charming towns and villages.

Later that week, near the end of the conference, I called his dispatcher to find out whether "Rye" would be available to take us back to London. When I mentioned his name, the dispatcher said "Who?"

"Rye," I said. "The driver who brought us here."

"Oh," the dispatcher replied, "You mean *Ray*."

Accents and regional slang expressions give away one's hometown, unless you've been away from home for awhile. In Michigan, for example, I've learned to refer to Pepsi and Coke as "pop" instead of its Wisconsin equivalent I grew up with, "soda." In most of the country, soda is the specific mix used with scotch, "club" soda, which has a completely different taste than the sweet soda flavor consumed in Wisconsin.

Other expressions I've found used only in southern Wisconsin towns are the words "once" tacked on to just any sentence (as in "come here once") and the concocted word "aina" which is used in place of "isn't it?"

Within striking distance of any military base, residents don't go to the bathroom; they head for the "head." And you'll hear a lot of "sirs" sprinkled into their conversational language. In the south, however, the word becomes "suh" and is used liberally by southern folks. Another southern tip-off term is the use of "daddy" in place of "father" or "dad"—who might also be called a "good ol' boy," but only by someone other than his own son or daughter. In some other parts of the country, he might be referred to as "yer ol' man."

. An Oklahoman I once worked with used to love "dermaters" (tomatoes) with his morning eggs. In the northeast, the same vegetable is known as "toe-mah-toes." Oklahomans and Texans are always "fixin" to take action (as in "I'm fixin' to go downtown to the bank") and stretching monosyllabic words into two syllables (put on your hi-at, boy, and let's grab some grub for the day-awg so we can hay-ad for home").

As they might comment in New England, ain't it great to be living in the "melting paht" of the world?

While you're listening to and observing other people around you in the waiting area, you're probably being sized up by someone else. Stop for a moment and think about the characteristics of your dress and your speech that provide clues to other people about where you're from.

What are some of the words and phrases you use that would spill the beans about your hometown?

1. _____

2. _____

3. _____

4. _____

5. _____

What are some of the things you wear that might give away your secret?

1. _____

2. _____

3. _____

Here are some words, terms, and phrases that will test your powers of listening and observation. See how many of them you can identify correctly: (Answers on page 113)

1. British word for cookie: _____

2. West coast term "grub'n" means: _____

3. British word, "bumbershoot": _____

4. Coffeehouse term, "double no fun": _____

5. Arkansas term, "Acts like his bread ain't done": ____
   _____

6. Single-word definition for term, "on account of": ___
   _____

7. Area known as "beltway": _____

8. Definition of Boston term, "frappe": _____

9. "Go to the packy" in Boston: _____

10. Another word for submarine sandwich: _____

Some words and terms that could only be New Yorkese:

11. Lawryuh _____

12. Gedoutahea _____

13. Pikshuhs _____

14. Schlepp _____

15. Soder _____

Answers to quiz questions above:

1. Biscuit
2. To eat, or "delicious"
3. Umbrella
4. Double decaf latte
5. Not quite with it
6. Because
7. Center of political activity in Washington, D.C.
8. Shake or milkshake
9. Pick up some liquor
10. Hoagie, or grinder
11. Attorney
12. Leave—or, "you're kidding"
13. Pictures
14. Mess around
15. Soda pop

Source: USA Phrasebook, Lonely Planet Publication

PART III
Tales Of My Travels

Whether you travel frequently or rarely, you're bound to encounter turbulent circumstances on the road now and then. These are a few of mine, to help you pass the time with a smile on your face.

19.

Site Unseen

I tell you naught for your comfort,
Yea, naught for your desire,
Save that the sky grows darker yet
And the sea rises higher.

— G.K. Chesterton

"**Y**our group will love it, sir," the voice on the other end of the phone said in an enthusiastic, persuasive tone.

"Just a short hour-long cruise across our beautiful harbor," she continued, "and your guests will arrive at a delightful Polynesian restaurant in a good mood, ready to enjoy a delicious dinner."

Site unseen, I booked arrangements for over 100 Chrysler Marine dealers and their spouses from my office in Hartford, Wisconsin, 2,000 miles from Redondo Beach, California, the location of our upcoming new product announcement meeting.

A few days earlier, my boss had wandered into my office in the middle of a routine Monday afternoon and handed me the assignment to arrange meeting room accommodations, cocktail and meal functions, and other details at a hotel he had selected in Redondo Beach. I accepted the responsibility—my *first* mistake—and asked him how soon I'd be able to get out to California to look at the meeting room and conclude other arrangements.

"You don't need to spend the travel money," he responded firmly. "Just handle everything with the catering people by phone." I nodded compliance (my *second* mistake) and started to jot down some notes to use when it was time to call the hotel.

A couple of days later, armed with basic specifications for the meeting, I dialed the hotel and asked for the convention catering department. A smiling voice came on the line, and we proceeded to walk methodically through my checklist. When I reached the "cocktails and dinner" entries, she offered a deviation from my original meeting plan.

"Instead of having them dine in the hotel, I've got a special package that's perfect for your dealers," she said. "It's our 'sunset cocktail' cruise. Your guests board *The Little Skipper* tug boat right at our dock at about 6 p.m., cruise at a leisurely speed across the harbor for about an hour, and dock at the 'Grass Skirt' Polynesian restaurant, where they'll have dinner waiting for them at 7. While on board our quaint little boat, they'll be served cocktails, beer, wine, and soft drinks, and then—after dinner—your guests will top off the memorable evening with Irish Coffees on board while they cruise back to our hotel at about 9 p.m."

Sounded terrific. Site unseen, I booked the cruise and dinner reservations.

Several months later, a day before the dealer meeting, our meeting team—including the general manager of our division, the sales and marketing managers, and a couple of additional staff members, including myself—set out for Los Angeles. We picked up a rental car at LAX and drove to Redondo Beach.

After checking in and dropping our luggage in our rooms, we headed down the escalator to survey the meeting facility. *Third mistake.*

The selected meeting room was the right size and configuration, but it included one feature the hotel coordinator had failed to mention, unbelievably, in our phone conversation. Right in the exact center of the room, which was decorated in a nautical theme, was a ship's mast that protruded from the floor and headed straight through the ceiling. It may have been appropriate to the decor, but it was far from compatible with our meeting plans, which included slide presentations we thought we'd make on a screen in the center of the stage. Our GM was the first to snarl.

"We've got to get us a better room," he said with a glint of emotion in his voice.

"This will never do. Didn't you ask about this when you booked the room?"

I shook my head apologetically. A few minutes later, we learned that the hotel was fully booked with other meetings and there were no alternative facilities on the premises. This is great, I thought. We were stuck with a white elephant meeting room and the boss thought it was my doing. The trip was off to a swell start.

We decided to reposition all of the chairs to one side of the room and point the projector diagonally over their heads to the left edge of the seating area where we placed the screen. Not an ideal solution, but one that would do under the circumstances.

The next morning, the dealers arrived and our day-long meeting went off without further hitches. Then it was time for our harbor cruise-slash-cocktail hour. We escorted the group to the dock and the dealers filed onto *The Little Skipper*, where they were greeted by a Dixieland combo, a fully-stocked bar, three eager bartenders, and a sumptuous hors d'oeuvres table.

All was well at that point, except that I noticed a line of clouds on the horizon and felt a slight breeze that was causing a few ripples on the surface of the water. As the last of the dealers climbed aboard, the band struck up a lively tune and our guests crowded around the bar as the *Skipper* backed away from the dock and headed out into the harbor.

Everyone seemed to be having a good time as the second round of drinks was served and consumed, but hardly anyone noticed that the clouds had moved closer to our location, the breeze began to turn into a wind, and the sea began to churn and rock the boat ever so gently. By the time the third round of drinks was completed, almost everyone noted that the tugboat was beginning to pitch and roll with more zest.

As the wind became more brisk and the first of our guests heaved their hors d'oeuvres over the side, I posed a private question in my mind: Could a true marine dealer who spends a lot of time on water get seasick?

A few moments later, my question was answered, and not so privately. First three, and then six, and then half the group was hanging over the gunwales, depositing the insides of their stomachs into the bay. The band stopped playing, but the bartenders went on serving to the hearty souls who thought that one more drink would settle the gyrating deck and smooth the journey. No such luck.

The winds grew more fierce, the sea rocked more strenuously, and the tugboat creaked as the captain revved the engines to counter the white-capped waves. We were now a full hour out of port and land was still a considerable distance away.

Some of the dealers ordered drinks, turned around from the bar, and spilled the contents of their glasses over their spouses or fellow dealers with whom they were engaged in conversation. We had a disaster on our hands. But, unbelievably, the worst was yet to come.

At about 8:30, two and one-half hours after we had left the hotel dock, we arrived at the restaurant. The crew tied up the boat to some pilings and extended a plank down to the dock. Anxious to get on solid earth, but hardly able to walk a straight line after the extended drinking period, the first few to disembark toppled off the plank into bait tanks adjacent to the dock. Together with my meeting team associates, I helped pull them out of the water and safely onto the dock.

As others looked after the dealers who followed, I sprinted up to the restaurant and hailed the manager.

"We're finally here," I announced. "We had a problem with the storm."

"I'm sorry, sir," he responded in a tone I didn't want to hear. "But we needed the reserved tables for our customers. When you hadn't arrived by eight o'clock, we released your tables, and we cannot accommodate you as a group. You'll have to split up at individual tables as they become available."

Having little (actually no) negotiating leverage, I agreed to his plan. The dealers filed in, wet, cold, and inebriated, and we got most of them seated within a half hour. Now I faced still another challenge.

Since the wind hadn't let up, how were we going to get over 100 people back to the hotel? I knew they'd commit mutiny if we tried to shove them back aboard *The Little Skipper*. Land transportation was the only solution.

I called every taxi company in the county and arranged for 65 cabs to pick up our guests as soon as the taxis could get to the front door of the restaurant. Each dealer had to pay the fare, but at that point they were glad to have any kind of alternative to the *Skipper* to return to Redondo Beach.

The next morning, everyone talked about the "sunset cruise." And, to my relief, most people laughed off the disaster that we (and an Act of God) had created—site unseen. Sales of our products during the order-signing session that followed breakfast were outstanding, and our continued employment was assured for another year.

Since that day, I've learned a lot of lessons in life. But two I follow most rigidly are:

1. I don't do group boat trips.
2. I don't book meeting facilities sight (or site) unseen.

20.

The Barber "Dun" It

Life is a jest; and all things show it.
I thought so once; but now I know it.

— John Gay

One of my bosses at Chrysler had the habit of using the preflight waiting time in airports to concoct practical jokes. He was the general manager of our division, and we traveled together frequently, along with the sales manager, engineering guru, and the marketing director. At that point of my career, I was the manager of advertising and sales promotion of Chrysler's Marine Division.

Ed, the engineering director, was an aggressively curious individual who frequently occupied himself with exhaustive investigations of his surroundings, learning all there was to know about them, and then wouldn't be able to determine where he had put his flight ticket. He was an ideal target for the general manager's practical jokes.

On a trip to San Diego, for example, Ed decided to get a haircut the morning of our departure back to Michigan. But, since his desire occurred spontaneously, the best he could do in

123

the selection of a barber shop was to find one close to the Camp Pendleton marine base. If you're already running ahead of me in this anecdote, you know that the marine barber trimmed Ed's hair rather close to the scalp. . . looking like he was fresh out of the service . . . or the penitentiary.

Besides evoking a good laugh from all of us when Ed rejoined the group, his appearance opened the door for an impromptu setup by the GM. After we boarded our flight, Ed became preoccupied (as usual) with something on the aircraft for a few minutes while the rest of us took our seats. Meanwhile, our boss, Don, motioned to the flight attendant that he wanted to speak with her. Acting very secretive and serious, he pointed to Ed and told the flight attendant that he was under our custody as a parolee being returned to civilian life in Michigan. Don said that since we were operating within strict rules, under no circumstances was the "ex-con" to be served any alcoholic beverages. The flight attendant nodded her compliance, and continued on with her routine chores.

As the preliminary preparations were being concluded in the flight cabin, Ed returned to his seat just in time to observe that we were enjoying double Tanqueray® martinis on the rocks, along with some crackers and cheese. The sight of the refreshments made him settle in quickly and prepare to join us in a cool libation.

He motioned to the stewardess. She ignored him. He motioned once again.

Still no response. Momentarily, she disappeared into the galley and reappeared with a pad, prepared to write down his order.

"Sir," she said while we sipped our premium gin concoctions, "would you like a soft drink, juice, or coffee?"

"None of those," Ed responded. "I want what they're having. One of those silver things. A double—on the rocks."

"I'm sorry, sir," she said. "I can only serve you soft drinks, juice, or coffee. Which one will you have?"

Still not catching on to our ruse, Ed sputtered, "I want a martini. One of those. Like that one right there."

When Ed's anxiety level reached a fever pitch, the head flight attendant appeared from out of the galley and handed Ed a "Kiddie Cocktail"—a Coke over ice with a cherry and a pink umbrella hanging on the rim of the glass. Finally, the light lit up in Ed's closely-shaven head and he knew that he had been "had."

That was the last time Ed the Engineer even thought of having his hair cut while on a business trip. But he did gain some measure of revenge by placing a curse of sorts on the practical-joking general manager.

In a subsequent dealer meeting in Great Gorge, New Jersey, the setup crew had rigged small amounts of gunpowder in tin cans at the front of the hotel stage. Then, they hooked up electrical impulse connectors that would set off the powder on cue, sending puffs of smoke into the air and creating a loud "Bang!" that would get everyone's attention when Don unveiled the new outboard motor models.

During rehearsals, the blast filled the room full of smoke and almost set off the sprinkler system—so I directed my assistant, Tom, to disconnect the apparatus. We would just have to rev up the audience without the special effect, I thought. But read on.

Because he had other details to attend to, Tom waited until just before the show to remove the wires and just barely finished when our first presentation began. Since he was in a hurry, Tom left the tin cans containing the gunpowder on the edge of the stage—thinking he'd retrieve the cans during the morning break.

Don, the general manager, went on with his presentation, doing his usual superlative job of exciting the dealers about our products for the coming year. Don laid on the blarney extra thick, in what was an almost flawless performance. Note the word *almost*.

During his concluding remarks, Don's adrenaline was running high and he inadvertently invited the group to join him on stage to view the motors up close. A cardinal rule of show business is that you keep the audience off the stage at all costs.

Because of the curse of Ed, the "parolee," Don broke the rule. In about 30 seconds, he was surrounded by dealers, all trying to get close to the new products at one time. Some wandered behind the stage set, trying to find out how our staging gimmicks worked. One of our biggest volume dealers had been sitting in the front row of the audience, so he surged forward at the head of the pack and, at the same time, kept one eye out for the nearest ashtray where he could douse the stogie that had been smelling up the meeting room.

Naturally, the closest container was the tin can with dry gunpowder. He submerged his cigar butt, into what appeared to be sand, and set off what seemed like a sonic boom. There were chandeliers shaking, workers running outside to find out what had hit the building, and general chaos. And then there was our cigar-smoking dealer.

The expression on his face would have been hilarious, had it not looked so odd. His eyebrows were missing, and the hair on his arm was burned to a crisp.

His mouth was open wide, as he assessed the damage. Naturally, the rest of the dealers stood around in stunned silence.

The general manager's wife, Jerrietta, was first to spring into action, grabbing him by the singed arm and moving him into an anteroom where we could have some privacy. After about 20 minutes of being ministered to, the dealer accepted our profuse litany of apologies, shook our hands, and went on his way with nary a mention of the "L" word (legal term meaning we could have been taken to the cleaners).

He thanked us for the day's entertainment, laughed about the incident, and kept on talking while we sneaked out the back door. The "curse" had caused the blast, but he miraculously had not experienced any serious physical effects of the junior explosion, except for the singed arms and eyebrows.

Don and the crew had an extra serving of Chivas Regal® during the post meeting reception. And there were no tin cans to be seen on stage in any of the ensuing (pardon the expression) meetings that summer.

At another meeting, the curse struck again when Don demonstrated a key feature of our outboard motors before a large crowd at Caesar's Palace in Las Vegas.

That year, the theme of our engineering was focused on cleaning up the exhaust emissions and minimizing pollutants left behind in lakes and rivers. To dramatize the clean water story, Don had us remove the powerhead from a 55 horsepower engine and replace it with a water cooler, which was hidden inside the powerhead cover.

Then, at a key point of the presentation, Don would walk up to the engine, grab a glass, and proceed to pour himself a cool drink of water from the concealed cooler.

He'd drain the glass in one long drink and continue with his description of the advancements that had eliminated the pollution threat.

Through five meetings in the series, the presentation went off without hitches.

For the tour's finale in Vegas, however, we decided to fill the cooler with ice cold vodka instead of water. As his routine reached the point where the demonstration took place, we all huddled in the dark behind the audience.

Don poured the liquid into his glass, toasted the crowd, and chug-a-lugged about four ounces of straight vodka down his throat, thinking that he was drinking water. The realization that he was not drinking water hit about two-thirds of the way through the glass. He pulled up suddenly, finished the rest of the drink by sipping it slowly, and glared at us in the back of the ballroom. Finally he spoke:

"I'll get you for thish!," he blurted. The audience, thinking he had been drinking clear water, had no idea what was happening. Don managed to get through the rest of his presentation without any noticeable slurring of his speech and we went to break.

Fearing the worst, we spread out throughout the room. True to form, however, Don took the episode in stride, came over to shake our hands, asked us to order a jar of olives from room service, and went on with the rest of the meeting like the trooper he was.

But that day marked the only time any of us could remember that the joker had been the subject of the joke. We all agreed: the curse was in fine form on that day.

And so was the joker.

21.

Adventure In Texas

Every man meets his Waterloo at last.
—Wendell Phillips

During the 15 years of my career in management positions with Chrysler Marine, I was the recipient of countless requests from hundreds of self-made promoters who prowled the telephone lines, with their hands outstretched, for donations of boats, motors, and equipment. Most of them were so obviously unqualified and phony, it was a simple pleasure to reject their requests out of hand.

One day, however, I reviewed a neatly-typed proposal that merited further scrutiny. It was from a fellow in Houston by the name of Doc Rail. In his letter, Doc wrote that he was the founder and head man of the Doc Rail water ski show in Galveston, Texas, at a place called Sea-Arama Marineworld, Galveston. He detailed his needs for equipment and described the broad range of promotional exposure our participation in his show would bring to our product line and brand name. Finally, he invited us to come down to Galveston to see the show first-hand before making a decision on his proposal.

I called Doc, discussed the terms of his request in greater detail, and accepted his invitation.

Our sales promotion manager, Jim Pryor, and the account supervisor of our business at Ross Roy Advertising agency in Detroit, Pete Vetowich, agreed to join me in evaluating the potential benefits of a relationship with Doc Rail. Jim and I flew down from Detroit Metro to Houston International and awaited the arrival of Pete, who was coming in from a photo shoot in Florida. The three of us met at a lounge near the arrival gate and decided to have a couple of drinks before picking up our rental car. Untypically, I ordered a Coke® rather than the usual cocktail, while my colleagues enjoyed a couple of Budweisers®.

When we finally headed over to the rental car counter, the decision as to who was going to rent and drive the car was a done deal in my favor, since I was the only one who had avoided alcohol. I accepted the role as a matter of course.

We dumped our bags into the trunk of the car, gathered up some maps, and headed out toward Galveston, on the main freeway through Houston. During the ride, a lot of conversation ensued about the ski show proposal and the potential opportunity it would offer to our company. We talked about the plusses and minuses of the "tradeout" in conversation that flowed freely, as I kept one eye on a map and another on the road.

After Pete alerted me to our upcoming turn-off, I eased our car onto the exit ramp and headed toward Webster, a Houston suburb, where we had booked hotel rooms for the overnight stay. I decelerated to about 45 mph and drove south along a two-lane road on the outskirts of Webster. Our conversation continued for a few more seconds, until I noticed a sudden movement out of the corner of my eye. I hit the brakes.

A police officer of some kind had darted out on foot toward the road from behind a billboard. He pointed toward the curb, so I pulled over. All conversation stopped as the officer moved aggressively toward our car and came around to the driver's side door.

As he approached, we all observed that he bore a striking resemblance to Don Knotts' deputy sheriff character on the popular *Andy Griffith* TV show. His huge, gold star badge on his starched tan shirt made him hunch over slightly as he walked or stood. In his shiny leather belt was a single polished silver bullet and a mini-revolver that had been carefully buffed so it gleamed in the late afternoon sun.

Finally, he spoke, and the resemblance grew even stronger. He had a high-pitched, tense voice that cracked periodically, like a teenage boy in a soprano choir.

I began to pull my driver's license out of my billfold and asked him the speed at which he had clocked me, but he cut me off in mid-question and ordered me out of the car—immediately if not sooner, according to his authoritative demeanor. As I climbed out of the vehicle, I heard a muffled chuckle coming from the back seat of the rental car.

The deupty's voice creaked and cracked as he demanded my license, and I complied without delay. He then explained that he had clocked me at 45 miles per hour. When I asked him for the speed limit, he pointed to a sign that marked the beginning of a school zone—on a line, approximately, with the billboard that had shielded him from us as we approached.

"But school's been over for more than three hours," I protested mildly.

"Don' make no never mind, boy," he responded. "Speed

limit's the same all day an' all night." By now, he had just about finished scribbling on the speeding ticket. Chuckling sounds continued in both the front and back seats of our rental car.

He jotted some additional details on the ticket, then said, "Boy, y'or goin' to have to come to the station and post bond or pay the fine, on account of yo'r under arrest," he proclaimed with a smirk on his face.

I said I'd follow him to the station in our car, but he wouldn't hear of it. As far as he was concerned, I was a virtual criminal—and a Yankee one at that, and he didn't want to give me any space. He opened the rear door of his dirt-covered sheriff's patrol car and I climbed in, while Pete and Jim were back in the rental car taking none of this seriously. I was suddenly isolated from them, by bullet-proof plexiglass, and the situation was getting more unnerving by the minute.

The deputy pulled out of the alley behind the billboard and made a big production out of arm-signalling Pete, who was now driving, to follow the patrol car to the station. We hadn't traveled more than 50 yards, when he turned abruptly into an alley alongside a brick building with a flag pole in front. We had officially arrived at the Sheriff's Office.

As Pete parked the rental car, the deputy guided me through an anteroom and led me behind a counter, where he told me to stand while he finished writing the ticket. When that was accomplished, he summoned a clerk—a portly woman with an adding machine under her arm.

She moved toward the counter and plugged the machine cord into a rusty wall socket. He mumbled something to her and she started punching buttons on the adding machine. By this time, Pete and Jim had entered the anteroom and were witnessing this surrealistic scene out of some Tennessee Williams award-winning play.

I looked at Pete. He smirked unsympathetically. A glance at Jim revealed that he was on the brink of convulsions.

At long last, the button punching ceased and the clerk ripped off the tape that had now stretched all the way to the floor. I anticipated the worst—$200? $500? Four figures?

"That'll cost you $35.00, boy," the clerk announced with a note of superiority in her voice. I reached into my billfold and quickly produced a $50.00 bill to take care of the fine. She meticulously counted out fifteen single dollar bills in change and handed the stack to me.

"The nex' time y'or in Webstuh you got to slow da-own, boy," the deputy advised as his voice cracked one last time.

"Don't worry, Deputy," I commented as my composure returned, "There ain't gonna be a next time—and if we're ever here again, you won't find me behind the wheel." I nodded toward the dueling hyenas in the anteroom.

Since that experience, I've been to Europe over 20 times. To Hawaii twice. To Venezuela, Mexico, and South Africa. But I ain't never set foot again in Webster. And I don't intend to, boy.

P.S. The ski show was great and we consigned a full line of boats and motors to Doc and his crew.

22.

What's The Big Idea?

*These success encourages: they can
because they think they can.*

—Virgil

I've always found that my creativity quotient tends to improve dramatically when I travel. Looking at my job from a broad perspective, without phones and faxes and normal interruptions, stimulates idea generation. I think that one of the reasons why my imagination flourishes while traveling is that there's no one around to tell me it can't be done—unlike the office environment, where everyone has some silly reason why it just won't work.

A good example of the creativity phenomenon occurred while I was on a trip to attend a *Business Week* strategic planning seminar in New York. Back at the office earlier that week, we had been unsuccessfully brainstorming new, branded product concepts. Our meetings, to date, had yielded nothing worth pursuing. (At FTD, a "branded product" was a special, nationally-advertised bouquet of flowers that could be replicated in any floral shop in North America—guaranteed—so you'd know by visiting your local florist what the bouquet delivered to your Grandma Harriett in Rochester would look like.)

During a break in my seminar, I strolled mentally through the challenge that we were dealing with and began to doodle on a writing pad at my meeting table. Some years back, the company had successfully marketed a bouquet called the "Forget-Me-Not" with commercials featuring Louie Jourdan, so I doodled alternative hyphenated groups of words that might lead to a possible suggestion of a viable product concept.

After a few minutes, the term "Pick-Me-Up" appeared on my list. I paused to reflect for a moment on the name and its potential meaning to a flower-buyer. In today's hectic world, everyone needs a "pick-me-up" once in a while, I reasoned, especially on a bad day. And, interestingly, it occurred to me that the ambiguous term could suggest the nature and form of the arrangement's container and package.

Feeling that I was on a solid path, I sketched out a rough drawing of a coffee mug with a handle, as a possible container in which the bouquet could be arranged.

Taking the concept one step further, I drew a carrying bag with handles as a possible packaging unit to replace the usual mundane florist method of wrapping an arrangement in paper or plastic. Hmmmmmm. A handle on the container and another on the carryout bag seemed perfect symbols of the "pick-me-up" idea.

Following my return to the office after the seminar, I turned the rough concept drawings and a product positioning brief over to the agency for further development.

They added a rainbow graphic to both the mug and the carry

bag and, after a few dozen meetings and about $100,000 worth of research, we were ready for market in the summer of 1984.

We introduced the new product at the 1984 FTD convention in Montreal and it was an instant hit with the florists. In the launch TV commercial, our spokesman, Merlin Olsen, appeared

in a football clubhouse talking to a player who had locked himself into a locker after fumbling the ball six times in the first half. Merlin commiserated briefly with the distraught player, then produced a Pick-Me-Up bouquet and extolled its features that just happened to include handles so it could be picked up without fumbling the arrangement. Prominent in the message was our positioning strategy, "For someone having less than a perfect day."

The product launch soon afterward went smoothly and we proceeded to sell almost 1.5 million Pick-Me-Ups in the first year, far exceeding our projections. And, the marketing campaign designed in collaboration with Mike Hogan and Rob Carr at D'Arcy Masius Benton and Bowles Advertising agency was recognized by the American Marketing Association, who presented us with their Gold "Effie" Award in 1985. Since that new product launch, FTD florists have sold over $200 million at retail in Pick-Me-Up bouquets, an all-time record in the floral industry.

Since my trip to the New York seminar in 1983, I have tried desperately to replicate the creative moments producing the successful product concept which led to the Pick-Me-Up bouquet. But I never have.

Nevertheless, I still find travel to be the best time for creative ideas to pop into my head. Incidentally, have I told you about this book concept I've developed? It would be a guide to enrich your waiting time in an airport. With brain-teasers, stories, tips . . . Nah, it'll never sell.

23.

Schmoozing
Within the Beltway

The Celebrity is a person who is known for his well-knownness.

— Daniel J. Boorstin

If you're in business, the idle time created by this delay in your itinerary provides you with the perfect opportunity to plan to do something you may not have thought about recently: thank your customers. After all, they are your true bosses and they're indispensable, so why not do something special for them this year?

As an advertising supporter of *The David Brinkley* Sunday morning news program in the early 1980s, I was invited along with the senior vice-president of our advertising agency to attend a "thank you" party in Washington, marking the first anniversary of the television program on ABC.

The celebration took place in the opulent accommodations of Washington's Watergate hotel, which is just a few short corridors away from the site of the Democratic headquarters break-in that ultimately toppled Richard Nixon from the presidential throne.

141

As I explained earlier, my upbringing on the south side of Milwaukee was very modest and I generally lead an average, low-key life. But suddenly, at this event, I found myself thrust into the middle of an esoteric discussion between Admiral Elmo Zumwalt, chairman of the Joint Chiefs of Staff; Roone Arledge, head of ABC News; and two of ABC's veteran news reporters, Sander Vanocur and Barry Dunsmore. A few moments later, my wife and I enjoyed a casual chat with Douglas Fraser, head of the world's most powerful union, the United Auto Workers.

As we strolled around the room, I was approached by a young man who seemed to feel the need to strike up a discussion with someone outside of the Washington Beltway. He introduced himself as Hodding Carter, and I recognized him as the chief State Department spokesman in the recently-resolved Iranian hostage episode that toppled the administration of Jimmy Carter (no relation) and put Ronald Reagan into office. Hodding was the lead player on the evening news night after night during the crisis.

While we talked pleasantly, Carter and I were joined by Helen Thomas, United Press International reporter who has been the lead-off questioner at presidential news conferences for over 30 years. After a couple of minutes, I found myself face-to-face with Ted Koppel of ABC's *Nightline*, a program born during the hostage crisis in Iran.

As we munched shrimp and sipped Chardonnay, Ted began to tell some fascinating "behind-the-scenes" stories about the program, and he captivated my attention for about five minutes. At that point, just as the stories were getting more interesting, we were distracted abruptly by a talkative lady who wanted to inspect my name badge to determine whether or not she had

discovered a major player in the business world. She was instantly disappointed with what she found (no surprise to me) and moved on to bother another group. Unfortunately, Ted Koppel had also moved on, and his stories went unfinished.

I looked over toward the woman who had caused the disruption and recognized her as Evelyn Y. Davis. Ms. Davis gained worldwide fame in the 1970s as a corporate gadfly who built a career on interrupting shareholder meetings, with spine-cracking questions directed at the likes of Henry Ford, Armand Hammer, Lee Iacocca, and other top brass in blue chip corporate America. Most of them probably experienced the same feeling of exasperation as I did when she displayed her disruptive manners in my presence. On the other hand, Ted Koppel was probably getting bored with our conversation anyway.

Following the anniversary party, I couldn't help but feel that the network had done a magnificent job of expressing their appreciation to their loyal advertising clients and I was convinced their largesse would pay off in long-term billings from the sponsors present at the reception. Since the program is still on the air more than a decade later, I suspect I was right.

As for Ted Koppel, his *Nightline* program gives him a daily opportunity to tell all the stories he wants to tell. And never again has he been interrupted by a lady in search of a celebrity name tag.

24.

The
Dream Came True

The dream, alone, is of interest. What is
life, without a dream?

— Edmond Rostand

Since my boyhood days back in the 1950s, I've harbored the same athletic fantasies as millions of other American males and longed for the opportunity to experience the thrills of being a major league ballplayer. For years, I lived with the realization that severe limitations in talent and skill would keep me from accomplishing my dream, so I substituted high school and college baseball and, later, co-ed softball games as my "fix" for never having had a chance to stride to the plate and rip a line drive into the right field seats at Tiger Stadium in Detroit.

At Christmas time in 1992, however, I was granted my one opportunity to mingle on the diamond with bona fide major leaguers. One of my presents for that holiday was a certificate from my wife, Nancy, for four days' participation in a Detroit Tigers

Fantasy Baseball Camp in February, just prior to spring training. In the weeks that followed my Christmas surprise, I worked out on my exer-cycle every day, swung a bat in my basement, and booked time in a racquetball court so I could throw the ball off the front wall and perform fielding exercises.

Our departure day finally arrived. On February 2, 1993, with about 40 other over-the-hill fantasy campers, I traveled by plane from frigid Michigan to the Tampa, Florida airport. From there, a bus transported all of us to Lakeland, home of the Tigers' spring training facilities. After checking in at the Lakeland Holiday Inn, we walked as a group over to the clubhouse, where we were greeted by the sight of a freshly-pressed Detroit Tiger uniform in each of our open lockers. Our names were stitched on the back, as were our chosen numbers (mine was 41, the number worn by Eddie Mathews, my favorite player with the Milwaukee Braves during my growing-up days in Milwaukee).

Our group leader introduced us to the coaches—all former Tiger players—and we were organized into teams of about 15 players each. My team was headed up by Steve Kemp, who played left field in the 1980s before he was traded to the White Sox for Chet Lemon—who coached one of the other teams in the camp.

Steve led us out of the locker room in full uniform and we began batting and fielding practice for the first time. I hadn't hit a baseball or caught a pop fly for over 20 years, when my boys were teenagers. But suddenly, here I was, batting and throwing and doing all the things that were so much fun when I was a youngster playing ball for 6 to 8 hours every day.

During the practice, some of the other coaches wandered over and introduced themselves. We got to shake hands with

Willie Horton, Mickey Lolich, Jim Northrup, Pat Dobson, Gates Brown, Jim Price, Chet Lemon, John Hiller, and others—along with old-time stars like Virgil Trucks and his catcher from the forties, Joe Ginsberg.

Soon our practice ended, and we took the field for the first of five intra-squad games. It didn't take long for me to experience my first thrill on the diamond—a scratch infield hit that helped ignite a seven-run rally in the second inning. Later, I lined a clean single over the pitcher's head and into center field for another hit, as we went on to dominate the opposing team, 15 to 3, in five innings of play.

When I called home that evening, from my room at the Holiday Inn, Nancy could detect the exuberance of a young boy in my voice as I described the day's triumphs.

The second day, our team was beaten by an equally-outlandish score, but we salvaged a hard-fought win in the second game and stood at two victories, one loss after two days of competition. I had three more hits in the double header, but my success at bat was offset by a dropped throw and a completely-misjudged pop fly at first base.

At the end of the third day, our team led the standings and earned the right to bat first in the camp finale, a game against the former Tigers.

The big event took place at Henley field in Lakeland, where Ty Cobb had once worked out the kinks in spring training many years before. Tickets had been sold for this game, and more than 3,000 fans—mostly senior citizens—turned out to root for the underdogs. The underdogs were decidedly us.

Having picked a number out of a hat, I came up second in the batting order against Jim Price, catcher for the World Champion '68 Tigers. Our leadoff hitter struck out on three pitches from Price, who threw with medium speed. So, suddenly, here was my moment.

As my name was announced on the public address system, I walked up to the right side of the plate and took some deep breaths to calm my shaky nerves. Fortunately, there were no relatives or close friends in the audience to "spook" me even more. But my nervousness subsided as I stepped into the batter's box to face the first pitch, which I took for a strike to get a feel for Price's velocity.

The second pitch was also in the strike zone, so I swung— a split-second late, unfortunately—and drove the ball past the third baseman, but about five feet foul.

"Oh and two," the umpire barked as I stepped out of the box and knocked the dirt out of my fresh new spikes.

Stepping back into the box, I felt more confident that I could at least make contact with Price's pitches. Wasting no time, he wound up and threw a couple of balls low and away. So now I was 2-and-2. The crowd was cheering mildly.

The fifth pitch was out over the outside corner, and I swung hard. The ball took off toward the hole between third and short and looked like it was skipping into left field. Unfortunately for me, however, the shortstop had been imported from the Florida Southern baseball team to play with the Tiger veterans, and he speared the bounder and made the long throw to first base—but about six feet over Jim Northrup's head.

My goal of getting on base was accomplished. Since we had over 40 players on our team, my near base hit represented my only time at bat before the local fans.

But my day at the ballpark concluded on a high note while I sat in the stands an inning later, munching a box lunch. One of the elderly fans, seeing me in my authentic Tiger uniform, ambled over and asked me for my autograph.

Now *that* made my day—and my career as a baseball player.

PART IV
Looking And Planning Ahead

Let's project ourselves into the future and prepare
for the best.

25.

To Prepare
Is To Succeed

I have seen the future, and it works.
— Lincoln Steffens

✈ ▬▬▬▬▬▬▬ Having endured the experience of being airport-bound—probably more than once—you need to prudently think ahead, anticipate that you're going to be stranded more than once in your lifetime, and formulate a plan for the next time around. Here are some strategies to consider:

1. Join an airline lounge club.
If you fly at least once per month, club lounge membership is a worthwhile investment that will pay dividends in the form of a comfortable, normally-quiet setting with facilities in which to work or relax.

The airline clubs are not for everyone. The cost ranges from $100 to $175, plus an initial fee of $25 to $100. For a spouse membership, add another $25 to $75. You (and an occasional guest) will enjoy "free" coffee, access to bar drinks at nominal costs, TVs, phones, computers and modem hookups, and storage facilities for your baggage and belongings. There

153

are no annoyingly disruptive public address announcements blaring from loud speakers; but, to ensure you don't miss your rebooked flight, an attendant is on duty to check your reservation, issue boarding passes, and page you discreetly if changes occur in your departure time.

Some downsides of club membership: The club you belong to may be located in the next terminal, hours of operation are limited, and the lounge may be crowded at times. One of the worst places for lounges is New York's LaGuardia on a Friday afternoon or evening; but then, the gate areas are even worse choices for relaxing while you await your departure at that time of the week.

One of the other perks I like about club lounges is that there's a dress code and you're not likely to have to look at the latest oil-skinned specimen from the body-building class, in his tank top and short shorts, for the next two hours. . . unless you want to, of course, in which case you will be better entertained in the gate area or at the fringe of the main concourse.

There is an air of haughtiness in the club lounge, since it is specifically designed to provide a measure of exclusivity (i.e. its stiff membership fees). But after your ears and eyes have been repeatedly battered by the cacophony of contemporary humanity that attempts to co-exist in any airport holding area, where the masses eat, drink, sleep, and often carry on as if there were no one else in the place, the comforts of an hour or two in the club lounge will justify the guilt of snobbery that is indigenous to such an establishment.

2. Buy a portable tape player.

For about $60, you can equip yourself with a good quality tape machine with a headset that will serve you well over many years of traveling. Bring along cassettes of your favorite music, with emphasis on softer selections that will help you relax. I like to record programs off my local radio station and play the tapes while I'm on the road, for two reasons: 1) They remind me of home, and 2) I can record up to 90 minutes on a single cassette, so I don't have to bring along as many as I would with shorter, commercially-produced tapes.

One additional benefit of having a tape player is that the headset puts a damper on ambient noise from cranky kids and the endless stream of announcements that flow out of the public address speaker system in any part of the terminal.

3. Travel with reading and writing materials.

Let's face it, the typical life of a working person today doesn't allow for a lot of private "thinking" time, much less time to reflect on one's past or future. Being holed up in an airport terminal, your own business or social universe temporarily out-of-touch with you, offers welcome opportunities to ponder life and to put a few things into perspective.

Reading about someone else's life and fantasies may, hopefully, spark a desire to put down on paper some thoughts, however superficial and rough at first, on your own life and times. Instead of trying to plow through the week's business correspondence during your airport layover, you'll find it much more enlightening and satisfying to jot down some thoughts about your life, your feelings, and those who have made you what you are.

4. Pack some personal entertainment.

Many adult travelers are unaware of the sheer entertainment value of hand-held electronic games, but they would be valuable allies if your flight delay is more than an hour. A friend of mine watched a fellow passenger amuse himself all the way from California to Detroit during one trip, and thought the fellow must have been a juvenile mentally—until he handed the game to my friend for a trial run. A *GameBoy*® with *Tetris* (his choice) costs about $60, but you can buy games like video poker for as little as $10.

5. Make reservations on non-stop flights whenever possible.

Every time your plane has to land and take off another opportunity is provided for some kind of problem that will leave you trapped in the airport without a way to get back on your original itinerary. Work with a travel agent to investigate all possible options to reach your destination with a minimum of connections.

If you have the flexibility to choose your approximate arrival time, select flights that arrive at times other than during prime early morning (7:30 to 9:30 a.m.) or late afternoon (4 to 7 p.m.) periods, the busiest traffic peaks in most airports.

Also, try to route yourself through less-populated intermediate cities if you can—for example, the bright new John Wayne airport in Long Beach rather than Los Angeles, or Billy Mitchell International airport in Milwaukee rather than through Chicago. This option may not fit into your itinerary but if it does, opt for the smaller markets where airport traffic is far more manageable.

6. Book seats in the emergency exit rows for extra leg room and comfort.

You'll have obligations to study the instructions in the seat pocket and will need to pay special attention to the flight attendants' directions, but the minimal effort you have to make will be more than offset by the substantial improvement in space between rows.

7. Make sure your travel agent has your preferences listed in your computer file.

If you favor aisle seats toward the front of the cabin, have your agent list that preference in their computer, so your needs will be considered each time they book tickets for you. Also, ask them to post your frequent flyer numbers in your file, so they'll be automatically entered on your tickets, saving you the chore of digging out your airline reference cards each time you fly. Another preference I like to have the travel agency accommodate is the notation that I favor non-smoking hotel rooms whenever they're available. Checking into a room previously occupied by a smoker gets my hotel stay off to a bad start, and my agents help me avoid the unpleasant experience by automatically booking non-smoking rooms whenever I travel.

8. Pack a small sampling of healthy snack foods and beverages.

Include low-fat, low-calorie foods that won't spoil and add a plastic bottle of water or juice in a carrier you can easily handle in a crowded airport terminal. And, don't forget to:

9. Order special meals.

Call the airline at least 24 hours before flight time and order low-fat, low-salt, low-calorie meals and you'll be pleasantly surprised at their quality and good taste. Fruit salads are especially refreshing, filling, and good for you. Several of the carriers offer "Heart Smart" menu entrees that will make you avoid both calories and guilt while in the air.

10. Put your stuff on wheels.

Today's traveler needs to be mobile and self-sufficient. When you pack for a trip, plan on taking along only the bare essentials so you can avoid checking in your baggage. And by all means, take it in a wheeled bag so you can pull it down the long terminal concourses, fold the handle, and carry it on board. You'll congratulate yourself many times over for having had the smarts to invest $60 to $150 in a piece of luggage you'll hardly ever have to carry.

The wheeled luggage carts made available at airports are always at the opposite end of the terminal from your drop-off point. And why fumble around in your pockets and purse for a couple of crisp, unbent dollar bills that will fit into the slot which unlocks the squeeky-wheeled cart, when you can avoid the hassle by putting your belongings on wheels from the beginning of your trip to the end. Wheeled luggage will pay for itself in reduced anxiety and physical strain.

11. Dress casually.

Unless it's absolutely necessary, avoid business suits with tight-fitting shirts and ties. Open your collar, dress with wrinkle-resistant fabrics, and wear the most comfortable walking shoes in your closet. If you need to be wearing dress shoes upon your arrival, keep them handy in your wheelie bag during your trip until your plane touches down.

12. Observe the simple tenets of travel.

Always arrive early at your airport of departure. There's no better way to start the trip rattled and disheveled than to arrive with less than 30 minutes before flight time. Everything you try to do from that point becomes confusing, frustrating, and stress producing.

Make it your personal rule to arrive at least one hour or more prior to flight time, because you'll need the extra time if any step in the process goes out of kilter. When you're in a hurry, there's **never** a parking space close; the baggage handler is **always** tied up with luggage being checked in by the Mormon Tabernacle Choir; and the line at the check-in counter is always as long as it would be at the rest room outside a convention of female bottled spring water-tasters.

If you violate the one-hour rule and arrive late, there are a few ways in which you can minimize your impending trauma. First, have your driver drop you off at the Arrivals door, rather than in the Departures area, where you'll likely encounter less traffic and congestion at most airports.

Second, don't stand in line at the check-in counter unless you need to buy a ticket and/or if you have more luggage than an aide for Lady Di. Wheel your luggage past the check-in counter, through the security checkpoint, and right to the gate—where it will not only be put on the plane last, but will likely come off the plane first at the other end of your trip.

Except in the most complicated of circumstances, the gate agents can handle your ticketing requirements right there. In addition, they are fully aware of your flight's departure status and your presence at the counter will ensure that they won't leave without you.

If you're a habitual late-comer, you'll want to be especially careful about prebooking seats when you make your ticket reservations. You (and your row-mates) won't want to be stuck in a middle seat when you're perspiring and breathing heavily from your sprint down the concourse to make your flight. So plan in advance and book aisle seats whenever possible.

Another common sense rule of travel is to never ever leave your keys in checked baggage. I stupidly violated that rule one night on a 20-minute flight from Lansing, Michigan to Detroit with only three passengers aboard. When I arrived in Detroit, I found out my baggage had decided to stay overnight in Lansing. Since my car keys were in the wayward bag, I had to rent a car to get to my home some 45 miles away, then drive back to the airport the next morning to turn in the rental car and rescue my own car, once I had retrieved my prodigal luggage.

Don't even think about leaving keys in your checked baggage.

The tips I've described above come from my own experiences. I'm a lot smarter when I travel now than when I began to fly occasionally in my mid-twenties. That's when I thought that a direct flight meant a non-stop flight and that the vichyssoise should have been warmed before serving. *Not!*

I'm hopeful that something you just read will make your next trip more comfortable, less stressful, and more fun. If it doesn't, I apologize—but, just between you and me, have you passed any S.A.T. tests recently? (Just kiddin', dude.)

26.

The Future Of Travel
Is Up in the Air

For I dipt into the future, far as human
eye could see.
Saw the Vision of the world, and all the
wonder that would be.

— Alfred Lord Tennyson

W hat are your expectations for travel in the 21st century? Some people envision planet-to-planet space journeys in sleek shuttle ships when they consider futuristic transportation; but the practical thinkers among us are more concerned with the ways in which the earth-bound travel industry will be able to make our business and pleasure trips more pleasant, fulfilling, and safe as we jet into the new millenium.

When we look ahead five to ten years from now, we can count on two certainties: 1) There will be more people traveling longer distances, and 2) There will be more ways than ever before to keep in touch with your home base and/or office.

The prediction that there will be more people tieing up our transportation systems is an easy one.

Travel has grown rapidly during the latter half of the 20th century, and there's no reason to believe the trend won't continue into the 21st. The world is steadily getting smaller, because of economic progress by the lower and middle classes of society and the availability of better ways to get around, whether you're planning to cruise over to Aunt Martha's on that newly-paved interstate highway or fly off to visit your daughter, who's teaching English in a Japanese elementary school. And as international communications continue to improve, especially through the Internet, there will be more incentive to visit each other's home turf. Another indicator is that young people today are less inhibited by air travel than previous generations—like those of my wife's uncle Adam, who could afford to fly anywhere in the world but is afraid his first flight might be his last. Adam, who is 82, envisions a fiery crash on his maiden takeoff; therefore, he wouldn't be caught dead (excuse the expression) in an airport, much less in a plane.

Communications will continue to play a major role in the growth of the travel industry. A newly-emerging concept—the universal phone number—will contribute significantly to our ability to "keep in touch" with our families and business associates. We are now able to apply to our telephone service provider for a "500" number which will stay with us for the rest of our lives—unless we opt to disconnect it voluntarily. When we travel, we can program the number to forward our calls to any phone, cellular phone, pager, or direct-dial fax machine in the U.S. and 200 other countries. (AT & T calls the new service True Connections®, but other providers will undoubtedly offer it as well in the future.)

Unlike previous phone number assignments, the 500 number will go along with us when we move from one part of the country to another. It will be OUR number at work and at home, or at any spot you happen to be in around the globe. Like it or not, we'll all be reachable anywhere, anytime.

If you think that will be a major advantage, consider the fact that we'll be a phone call away from bill collectors and telemarketers while cruising in a Venetian gondola or scaling Mount Everest. Of course, there'll always be "Caller ID" to screen unwanted calls at the touch of a button.

Where's Greta Garbo ("I Vant to Be Alone") when we need her?

*   *   *

In addition to phone communication improvements, we can expect growth in the use of airport terminal facilities for tele-conferencing. Satellite uplinks and downlinks are now standard equipment at major airports, where meeting participants are able to land in the morning, participate in a teleconference involving sites all across the globe, and jet back home before sunset. Many such "meetings" are already taking place daily in some parts of the world.

The use of satellite communications will also impact on ordinary travelers as well. Before long, we'll all be wearing multi-function wristwatches that will, by way of satellites, access the weather report from the destination city and transmit messages back to the family without requiring the wearer to take a single step.

If you don't get turned on by the wristwatch communications link concept, you will be by the PDA (Personal Digital Assistant) device. A number of these hand-held mini computers are already on the market and their usefulness is expanding daily. The Apple Newton®, for example, will transform hand-written notes into typed copy, keep your calendar, datebook, and financial records up to date, and beam a phone number listing to your telephone, automatically dialing the number for you. The beaming device can also be used to communicate a message across a board room table to a compatible PDA. When you get to your office or home computer, you can download from the PDA to the computer or vice-versa.

And what about airports of the future? A spokesman for BAA, the British-based company that claims the title of the world's biggest airport operator, recently reported in *USA Today* that their corporate goal is to turn the airport terminal into "a pleasurable part of the journey." (Novel idea.)

BAA—formerly known as British Airport Authority—envisions future airports resembling a kind of Disneyland more than the passenger clearinghouse many terminals are now. That means we'll see more entertainment, more creature comforts, and more sensitivity toward customer needs. The British company is a leading proponent of privatizing airport operations, and is currently managing the Pittsburgh and Indianapolis airports in the United States, with more to come.

With their retailing and general business experience, BAA is attracting top names like GAP and Speedo to open airport terminal shops, encouraging travelers to part with more dollars while on their way to or from their flight gates. And it's working.

Average spending by passengers has more than doubled in airports run by BAA in the past five years. Even upscale stores like Harrods and Waterstone's Booksellers have opened outlets in Britain's seven BAA-run airports.

What about business travelers who don't have the time or inclination to shop in an airport? Several airlines are creating mini-business centers that enable the briefcase-carrier with a heavy workload to be productive while awaiting a flight. At LaGuardia airport in New York, for example, passengers booked on a USAir shuttle can meander to a gateside cubicle and work on an IBM Thinkpad® or Mac Powerbook® computer, have access to printers and fax machines, or catch up on the latest business magazines or papers. Snacks and refreshments are also available in these mock offices.

Gateside services are a coming trend that will undoubtedly expand as business travelers try to squeeze 25 hours into each day.

Finally, there is simply no way for us to judge the impact the computer will have on future travel. Most of us have underestimated its potential thus far, and others keep their heads buried in the sand, hoping the computer age will go away peacefully. But it's here to stay and to those who appreciate its positive points, we ask, "How in the world could we have functioned without it?"

To get some semblance of how it could impact our travel habits in the future, let's examine the service called "Travelocity®" offered on the World Wide Web. This futuristic program gives users the option to click on an icon labeled "3 Best Itineraries" to locate flight options ranked according to price, time, airline, and nonstop availability—options selected earlier by the users. The information requested pops on the screen immediately and offers the opportunity to order flight reservations—as well as view photos, video clips, maps, and event information and background for about 160 featured cities and regions.

Business travelers easily access addresses and phone numbers for messenger services, conference centers and computer rentals.

Travelocity is just one early example of the cyberspace approach to travel arrangements. There will be dozens of new programs available in the next year or two, and each new generation will be better, faster, and more convenient than its predecessor.

That's just a limited preview of the future of air travel. Think of the exciting things we'll be able to do with our waiting time in the years ahead!

27.

My Best To You

As the Spanish proverb says, 'He, who would bring home the wealth of the Indies, must carry the wealth of the Indies with him.' So it is in traveling; a man must carry knowledge with him, if he would bring home knowledge.

— Samuel Johnson

In my 30-plus years of travel all over the globe, I've experienced many top-notch cities, hotels, dining rooms, taxicabs, scenic views, and generally interesting places. In this closing chapter, I'm going to share my choices of the best in each loosely-defined category so that 1) You might seek out and enjoy the same kind of quality experience, if you're so inclined, or 2) You will be encouraged to put together a list of your own favorites and, in the process, relive some of the best days of your traveling life. Here's **my** "best of everything":

BEST CITY

Montreux, Switzerland, is my choice for the best place to which I've ever traveled. Its scenic settings are spectacular; its people are warm and friendly; its food is excellent, and then some; its activities are diverse and multi-cultured.

In our room at the Hotel Eden au Lac on Lake Geneva in downtown Montreux, we could throw open the window shutters and reveal the most picturesque setting imaginable: the snow-capped Alps in the background, the late spring greenery at the lower levels of the mountains, the shimmering lake in the fore-ground, its surface broken only by the occasional ferry boat mov-ing left to right or right to left across our horizon. In the imme-diate foreground was the beautifully landscaped and flowered shore walk that is tended by 3,000 local resident volunteers on a daily basis. Montreux is the site of the world's most famous jazz festival every July, attracting artists and audiences from all over the world. When I checked the scheduled performers for the summer following my visit, I found many classic jazz artists listed, as well as a familiar name I least expected: Renowned American jazz singer Johnny Cash. (Some booking agent didn't quite finish all of his or her homework.)

Almost as memorable as our stay in Montreux were the side trips we made to the Castle of Chillon, made famous by Lord Byron, and to the charming old village of Gruyeres in the mountains.

From Montreux, you can travel to Germany, France, Italy, Austria, and Greece in a matter of a few hours, especially if you take advantage of their superb rail system. But if you have an opportunity to stay in Montreux, why would you want to go anywhere else?

BEST U.S. CITY

I started traveling to **San Diego** in the late 1960s and have watched it change on every trip there since, and not always for the better. But despite its flaws and problems, this is the American city that I always hate to leave.

It has so much going for it. A wonderfully temperate climate. Interesting topography. Beautiful water vistas. Marinas. Major league sports. Plays and symphony concerts. A wide range of restaurants. Beaches. Shopping. Point Loma. Some of the finest hotels, including the world-famous Hotel del Coronado. The Zoo in Balboa Park. The adjoining towns, including La Jolla. And more.

In the 1970s, we set up annual "ride and drive" demonstrations for boating writers from all around the country in Mission Bay, a location that provided the writers with spectacular photo backgrounds as they put our new products to the test. The resulting coverage always exceeded our expectations.

And so does the city. After tourists spend weeks exploring the highlights of this beautiful area, they can—for contrast—head south to Tijuana, Mexico. But when I'm in San Diego, I'm where I want to be, and Tijuana ain't San Diego.

BEST HOTEL

The **Ritz-Carlton in Naples, Florida**, wins this election hands down. Everything at the Ritz is done exactly right, from the moment you pull into the driveway to the reluctant minutes you spend pausing before your departure. Every employee knows and uses your name as you move about the property and seek their assistance. The facilities are opulent but comfortably so;

the food is prepared by the finest of chefs; and the place is simply everything you've ever asked for in a hotel or the area in which it is located.

BEST SETTING

After a stay at the Hilton Hawaiian Village in Honolulu, we capped off our week of business meetings and sightseeing adventures by attending **Mass on the beach** near our hotel. The service featured Hawaiian hymns and dancers, with the whispering surf in the background. The altar was positioned so that the ocean served as a panoramic stage for the enchanting service. As the priest led us in prayer, we lost some of our concentration as we looked out over the rolling surf and followed the colorful sailboats dancing lazily on the horizon. But we learned, at the same time, to appreciate the spectacular beauty of one of God's finest creations. It was a magnificent, inspiring experience that we will long treasure.

MOST INTERESTING RESTAURANTS

If you've never had a handsome waiter from Poznan, Poland, break out into a full-voiced tenor presentation of an aria from the *Barber of Seville* between the antipasto and main courses, you've never been to the **Prima Vera** restaurant.

This is a fine Chicago favorite where the entire wait staff consists of trained and talented opera singers, accompanied by a pianist who is as adept at interpreting Puccini as he is polishing off the score of a Broadway show-stopper pop tune. While on their way to pick up yet another tray of exquisite pasta dishes, the soloist waiters and waitresses frequently burst into song or join with their colleagues for a duet or trio ensemble presentation.

One of the highlights of our experience at Prima Vera was the unique celebration of my wife's birthday, which was heralded by a stirring rendition of "Happy Birthday" lyrics set to the score of a brief extract from Handel's Hallelujah Chorus, sung lustily by a half-dozen waiters and waitresses who gathered around our table. A single, lighted candle in a slice of chocolate mousse pie added the only missing touch of class that capped off a beautiful weekend in the Windy City. Prima Vera is meant to be experienced only when you're in the mood for an extraordinary evening of fine food and fabulous entertainment— whether or not you're celebrating someone's birthday.

And if you're not, what the heck? Celebrate someone else's big occasion.

* * *

And then there's the breakfast at the **Swan Court** in Hawaii. Any meal at the Swan Court in Maui's Hyatt Regency hotel is an unforgettable pleasure, but breakfast is an especially delightful experience. In typical Hawaiian fashion, the dining room is an open-air facility, with a large exposure to the outdoors that enables diners to look out onto a beautifully landscaped pond, where graceful white swans cruise effortlessly from bank to bank, providing entertainment to customers while they polish off their eggs benedict. The food is excellent, but the real attraction is the spectacular setting.

Outside the Swan Court is an atrium walkway that features a selection of typically Hawaiian foliage, inhabited by bright and colorful birds of many tropical species. Of special interest are the multi-colored parrots, who chat with the visitors as they stroll toward the hotel lobby. The experience lets you relive a scene from *South Pacific*, and your expectation is that Mitzi Gaynor will appear from behind a banyan tree and break into a rendition of "Gonna Wash That Man Right Outta My Hair" before your very eyes.

* * *

Finally, you'll think you're seeing double at **New York's Twins** restaurant, but your condition has nothing to do with your alcohol consumption. It's just a result of their staffing policy which requires that all 30 waitresses, bartenders, hostesses, and doormen are identical twins. That means you can count on service that's twice as good as anywhere else, and you're expected to tip accordingly.

Of course, you can get yourself in the mood by having some kind of cocktail or mixed drink—double, of course—before dinner. The toughest part will be deciding who's going to listen to your joke at the bar—bartender Ted or bartender Fred.

On the other hand, you should be able to count on twice the laughs after you double the emphasis on the punch line.

MOST INTERESTING DRIVE

While on a trip to the island of Maui, we decided to check out the famous **Hana Highway**, the only land route to the village of Hana from the populated areas of the island. The deceptively-named "highway" provides you with 30 miles or so of winding, narrow road so perversely laid out that you rarely can exceed speeds of 20 miles per hour along the way. But why travel any faster, when some of the world's most scenic settings, including waterfalls, streams, colorful birds, and exquisite foliage await you at every turn? When we finally arrived in Hana, twisting and turning and gawking along the entire route, we were ready for a break that included a dining experience at the Hana hotel.

A view of the tropical forest provided the background setting for our meal. The menu, as you might expect, was dominated by seafood and fruit selections, all fresh and delicious. The Hana hotel is one of the most out-of-the-way tourist establishments we have ever encountered, but it was well worth the laborious trek.

BEST ENTERTAINMENT

We've been blessed with opportunities to enjoy the talents of many entertainers and artists during our travels over the years, from the stages of Las Vegas to the concert halls of Europe. But the night that stands out most in my recollection was the evening we were entertained by Pete Fountain, jazz clarinetist extraordinaire, and his band at **Pete Fountain's Club in New Orleans**.

The exceptional night of fun began with a wonderful dinner at Commander's Palace, famous for mint juleps and outstanding food. Then it was on to Fountain's, where Pete and the band played all of the classic jazz tunes for two hours or more. And, finally, we capped off the evening with a couple of Beignets at a cafe in the French Quarter.

MY FAVORITE RESTAURANT

Typical of many business travelers, I've dined in the best of restaurants and I've managed to be unsuccessful in dodging the worst. But for overall food quality, preparation, presentation, ambiance, and table service, my favorite place is **Tapawingo** in northern Michigan. Located on a small lake in the rural four-corner town of Ellsworth, Tapawingo not only attracts discriminating diners from everywhere, but also chefs from just about anywhere.

The chefs come to share ideas with, and learn from, Chef/Owner Harlan Peterson and Executive Chef Rich Travis of Tapawingo, two of the most-respected gourmet food experts in the midwest. Diners come to enjoy superb ambiance and extraordinary selections, spectacularly presented. And they frequently come back for more.

A typical Tapawingo menu includes appetizers like Molasses Cured Duck Taco with Green Chili Grits and Spicy Ancho Crusted Scallops served on a Thai slaw and soba noodles. If you aren't familiar with the exotic selections, don't worry—they're all delicious.

Principal dishes might include Lamb with Eggplant Timbale and Wok-Seared Whitefish with red chili pasta, macadamia nuts, and black sesame seeds.

As for ambiance, the cottage-style restaurant—a converted lakeside home built in the 1920s—is surrounded by colorful perennial gardens in the summer, available to arriving diners who also enjoy strolling across the back lawn down to the lake shore.

In 1995, *Gourmet* magazine rated the restaurant as one of ten rural dining establishments in the U.S. "with truly extraordinary cuisine."

You may prefer your own favorite spots from New York, Boston, San Francisco, or even Paris. That's understandable, but don't look for me there. I'll be at Tapawingo as often as possible. . . and whenever my budget allows. Reservations and directions: (616) 588-7971. Call several weeks in advance, especially in summer months.

BEST TAXICABS

Sorry, New York. Your taxi drivers sometimes take the long route to pad the meter, bellow profanities at other drivers, and clear their streaky windshields with Brillo pads.

Like most frequent travelers, I've enjoyed riding with some excellent cab drivers in my travels over the years. But I've also had the misfortune to be subjected to some of the worst, including these:

The cabbies in Stockholm and Rome who wear out the horns of their vehicles before their brake linings show even the slightest bit of consumption;

The New York cabbie who took us from mid-Manhattan to LaGuardia airport through the roughest part of Harlem on a hot summer day and, inadvertently, positioned us in the middle of a developing "street rumble" complete with broken wine bottle weaponry;

The Dusseldorf, Germany, taxi driver who cruised the Autobahn at 200- kilometers-an-hour in soup-thick fog to get us to downtown Cologne, where he became hopelessly lost because the fog prevented him from reading street signs.

The **best cab drivers** we've encountered in our years of travel were in **Chicago** and **London**. Chicago has some of the finest veteran drivers who demonstrate good manners, strong midwestern ethics, and a positive attitude that gives their passengers good feelings about them and their city. As good as they are, however, they still can't beat the overall standard of excellence demonstrated by taxicab drivers in London, England.

First of all, they take pride in maintaining spotless, well-appointed vehicles and in their own dress, which is both genteel and clean. Shoes are brightly-polished. In some U.S. towns, by contrast, the drivers look like they've just completed a thorough spring cleaning of a coal-burning furnace minutes before they pulled up at the curb.

Finally, the demeanor of the London cab drivers is formal, respectful, and uplifting to the passenger. When you see one of their all black Darth Vader-like vehicles approaching on a narrow London side street, it's a good idea to retreat to the safety of the sidewalk. But don't fear for your life, as you might in New York or Paris where curb-hopping is commonplace. London drivers are respectful of pedestrians, too. What'll they think of next?

*   *   *

The preceding selections were mine alone, based on my own carefully concocted criteria. You may have entirely different tastes, needs, and interests (and probably will), and you may hate the places I've loved. My point in bringing you this chapter is to stimulate your thinking about getting up and doing something. . . taking action rather than passively vegetating in front of the TV tube.

Whether your financial resources are modest, in good shape, or in the no-worry class, there are many things that can be done to put liveliness and interest into your life through travel.

I learned a long time ago, however, that just talking about it doesn't get you there. Wishful thinking was something appropriate for me to do while I sat next to my brother Jim on that rusted old running board of my dad's Zephyr.

Planning, and then executing the plan, gets it done.

Life is to be lived.

Live it today, and enjoy the memories tomorrow. . . even if they include periodic episodes of waiting in an airport.

We'll Smile and Lick the Spoon

Life's full of unplanned twists and turns
And who can say what's coming next?
We trudge our way through every day
As if our dismal, dreary lives were "hexed."

Then one day light bulbs shine so bright,
Our eyes are opened—not a moment too soon!
We endeavor to savor life's countless flavors,
And when it ends, we'll smile and lick the spoon.

Who's to say what's coming next?
A life of colorful pictures or mundane text?
Let's make the most of life today
And treasure its beauty in every way.

—Harry Knitter

APPENDIX I

North American Airlines' Toll-Free Numbers

AIR CANADA: 1-800-776-3000

AMERICA WEST: 1-800-235-9292

AMERICAN AIRLINES: 1-800-433-7300

AMERICAN EAGLE: 1-800-433-7300

CANADIAN AIRLINES: 1-800-426-7000

CONTINENTAL AIRLINES: .. 1-800-525-0280

DELTA AIRLINES: 1-800-221-1212

MIDWEST EXPRESS: 1-800-452-2022

NORTHWEST AIRLINES: 1-800-225-2525

SOUTHWEST AIRLINES: 1-800-435-9792

TWA: 1-800-221-2000

UNITED AIRLINES: 1-800-241-6522

UNITED EXPRESS: 1-800-241-6522

USAIR: 1-800-428-4322

APPENDIX II

Major Hotel Chains' Toll-Free Numbers

BEST WESTERN: 1-800-528-1234

CLARION: 1-800-221-2222

COMFORT INN: 1-800-221-2222

COURTYARD by Marriott: 1-800-321-2211

DAYS INN: 1-800-325-2525

EMBASSY SUITES: 1-800-EMBASSY

HAMPTON INN: 1-800-426-7866

HILTON: 1-800-HILTONS

HOLIDAY INN: 1-800-HOLIDAY

HOWARD JOHNSON: 1-800-GOHOJO

HYATT REGENCY: 1-800-233-1234

LA QUINTA: 1-800-531-5900

MARRIOTT: 1-800-228-9290

RADISSON: 1-800-333-3333

RAMADA: 1-800-2RAMADA

SHERATON: 1-800-325-3535

APPENDIX III

Rental Car Companies' Toll-Free Numbers

ALAMO: 1-800-327-9633

AVIS: 1-800-831-2847

BUDGET: 1-800-527-0700

DOLLAR: 1-800-800-4000

ENTERPRISE: 1-800-325-8007

HERTZ: 1-800-654-3131

NATIONAL: 1-800-227-7368

THRIFTY: 1-800-367-2277

APPENDIX IV

Bag Tag Codes

AOO: Altoona, PA
ANC: Anchorage
ATL: Atlanta
BOS: Boston
CLT: Charlotte
ORD: Chicago
CVG: Cincinnati
CLE: Cleveland
CMH: Columbus, OH
DFW: Dallas/Ft. Worth
DEN: Denver
DTW: Detroit Metro
FLL: Ft. Lauderdale
GRR: Grand Rapids, MI
IAH: Houston Intercont.
IND: Indianapolis
JAX: Jacksonville
MCI: Kansas City
LAN: Lansing
LAS: Las Vegas

LAX: Los Angeles Int'l.
SDF: Lousville
MKE: Milwaukee
MSP: Minneapolis
YUL: Montreal
EWR: Newark
MSY: New Orleans
JFK: New York Kennedy
LGA: New York, La Guardia
SNA: Orange County, CA
MCO: Orlando
PHL: Philadelphia
PHX: Phoenix
PIT: Pittsburgh
PDX: Portland
SLC: Salt Lake City
SEA: Seattle
YYZ: Toronto
IAD: Washington Dulles
DCA: Washington National

INDEX

ORDER FORM

Please send ___ copies of *Holding Pattern* to:

Name: _____

Address: _____

City: _____ State: _____ Country: _____

Zip Code: _____

Telephone Number: _____

Fax Number: _____

Price

$9.95 ea. plus $3.50 shipping and handling per book.
Five copies or more: $2.00 shipping and handling per book.

Michigan residents add 6% sales tax.
Outside United States: $13.00 ea. plus $5.00 shipping and handling per book.

Payment

1. Send check or money order (payable to *Kordene Publications)* for full amount to:
    Kordene Publications, Ltd.
    P.O. Box 776
    Okemos, MI 48805-0776
2. Credit Card Orders:
    _____VISA_____MasterCard
    Card #: _____
    Expiration Date: _____
    Signature:_____

Fax Orders

(800)STUCK77. Use this form.

Phone Orders

(800)879-4214. Please have your credit card ready.

Postal Orders

Mail to: Kordene Publications, Ltd.,
P.O. Box 776, Okemos, MI 48805-0776, USA

A portion of the proceeds of this book will be donated to the
American Parkinson's Disease Association.

Dear Reader:

I hope that *Holding Pattern* made your waiting time more enjoyable—or at least more bearable.

If you have stories about your own travels that you'd like to share, please send them to me at:

P.O. Box 776
Okemos, MI 48805-0776

I may use your story in my next book. If so, you'll be among the first to receive a copy—with my compliments and my autograph.

Thanks for making *Holding Pattern* a part of your life.

Harry Knitter
Author